BEYOND
THE MYTH

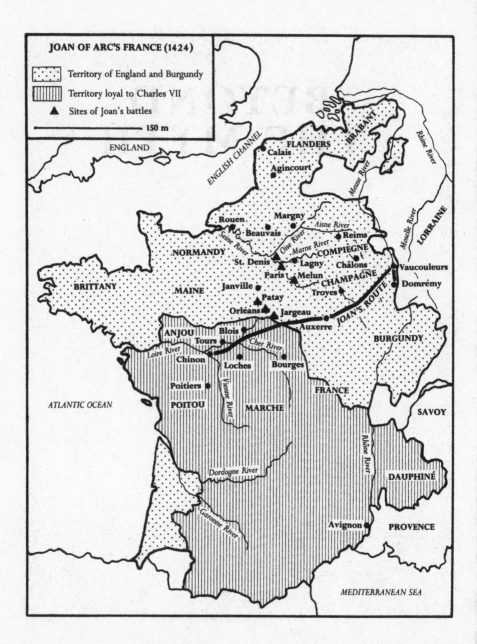

JOAN OF ARC'S FRANCE (1424)

Territory of England and Burgundy

Territory loyal to Charles VII

▲ Sites of Joan's battles

150 m

ENGLAND

ENGLISH CHANNEL

FLANDERS

BRABANT

Rhine River

Calais

Agincourt

Meuse River

Rouen

Margny

Aisne River

Moselle River

LORRAINE

Beauvais

Seine River

Oise River

Marne River

Reims

NORMANDY

St. Denis

Lagny

COMPIÈGNE

Vaucouleurs

BRITTANY

MAINE

Paris

Melun

Châlons

CHAMPAGNE

Domrémy

Janville

Troyes

JOAN'S ROUTE

ANJOU

Patay

Orléans

Jargeau

Auxerre

BURGUNDY

Blois

Tours

Cher River

FRANCE

Loire River

Chinon

Loches

Bourges

SAVOY

ATLANTIC OCEAN

Poitiers

Vienne River

MARCHE

Rhône River

POITOU

Dordogne River

DAUPHINÉ

Garonne River

Avignon

PROVENCE

MEDITERRANEAN SEA

BEYOND THE MYTH
THE STORY OF JOAN OF ARC

POLLY SCHOYER BROOKS

HOUGHTON MIFFLIN COMPANY
BOSTON

Library of Congress Cataloging-in-Publication Data
Brooks, Polly Schoyer.
Beyond the myth: the story of Joan of Arc/Polly Schoyer Brooks.
p. cm.
Summary: Places the life of the fifteenth-century girl who has
become a French national symbol within the social, religious, and
political context of her time.
PAP ISBN 0-395-98138-7
ISBN 978-0-395-98138-2

1. Joan, of Arc, Saint, 1412–1431 — Juvenile literature. 2. Christian
saints — France — Biography — Juvenile literature. 3. France —
History — Charles VII, 1422–1461 — Juvenile literature. [1. Joan,
of Arc, Saint, 1412–1431. 2. Saints. 3. France — History —
Charles VII, 1422–1461.] I. Title.
DC103.5.B76   1990
944'.026'092-dc20   89-37327
[B] CIP [92] AC

Printed in the United States of America
DOH 16
4500781059

To my daughter,
Joan Brooks McLane

CONTENTS

Contents

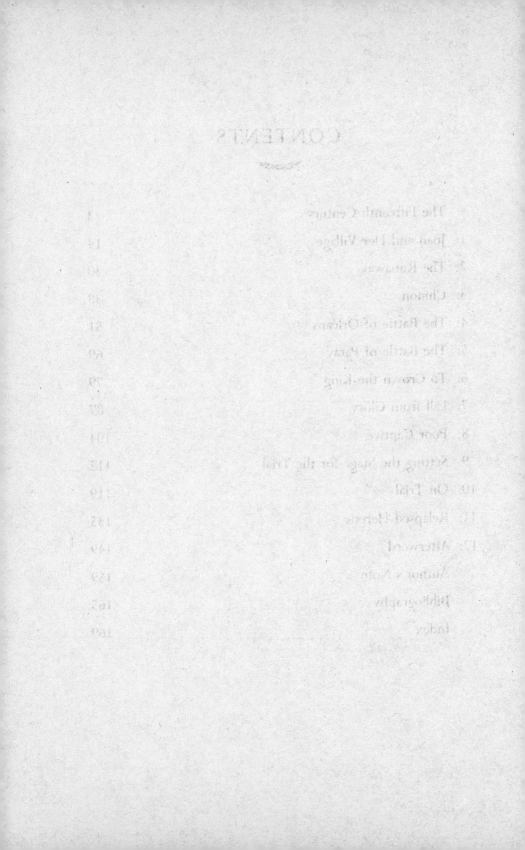

BEYOND THE MYTH

THE FIFTEENTH CENTURY

"There is great misery in the land of France."

The King was going mad. On a stifling hot day Charles VI of
France and his companions-in-arms rode out of the forest to
an open sandy area where the sun beat down unmercifully.
Suddenly he stopped and shuddered at the sound of steel clanging
on steel as a spear, dropped by his sleepy squire, struck a
helmet dangling from a saddle. In a panic the King rose in his
stirrups, drew his sword, and shouted "Traitors!" as he began
slashing wildly about. No one could stop him, and soon several
of his bodyguards lay dead. At last worn out by his own frenzy,
the King collapsed. Removed from his horse, he lay motionless
on the ground, unable to speak or to recognize anyone. Some
feared he had been poisoned, others that he had been bewitched.

This was the onset of insanity, and was followed by increasingly
frequent attacks. When sane, the young King was full of remorse
over the terrible things he had done and begged his courtiers
to hide all his weapons when they suspected a fit was coming
on. Sometimes he fancied he was made of glass and refused
to let anyone near him lest he be shattered to pieces. Such

was the pathetic King of France who reigned at a time when his country was at war and was ravaged by famine and disease, a time that cried out for leadership.

The frivolous, seductive Queen, Isabella, was of no help to her deranged husband. She led him on a round of wild, late-night parties and managed to have many love affairs on the side—no one was quite sure whether the King had fathered all of her eleven children. She was reputed to be the mistress of the King's younger brother—handsome, debonaire Duke Louis of Orléans. A playboy and a womanizer, Louis was also suspected of dabbling in sorcery and the arts of black magic. But his real interest was power. He longed to gain control of the mad King and to rule in his place. This ambition brought him headlong into conflict with an even more power-hungry member of the royal court, his cousin the Duke of Burgundy.

Despite his charms, Louis was no match for the Duke of Burgundy, the richest man in all the kingdom. Aptly called John the Fearless, he was one of the last of the powerful medieval dukes, and owned vast estates both in France and in Flanders, where he controlled a profitable wool trade with England. His court was the wealthiest and most luxurious in France, setting the style in manners and dress for all aristocrats. Like all powerful dukes, he was more feared than loved by the common people, who preferred the King to any feudal duke. Dukes had the reputation of being oppressive, of demanding hard labor and payment in exchange for protection, whereas the King was the symbol of justice and mercy. People looked to the King as their real protector against the harsh exactions of their local lords; they had the right to appeal to the King over the heads of their lords, over the heads of barons, over the heads of dukes, who all owed allegiance to the King. Kings had been gaining power over the last centuries but when kings were weak, ambitious nobles like John the Fearless might overstep their place in society and even overshadow the King in power and wealth. Still the King retained a special glory none of his vassals had—he was anointed with holy oil and crowned by the Church, which gave him an aura of sanctity and earned him the people's respect and loyalty.

Duke John the Fearless was as eager as Louis to take advantage of the King's insanity. Tension and rivalry between the cousins grew to violent hatred. Cruel and crafty, Duke John would stop at nothing to further his own interests. Late one night he sent a gang of thugs to waylay and murder Duke Louis as

Murder of the Duke of Orléans. Note severed hand lying by his blood-streaked head. Miniature painting. Bibliothèque Nationale, Paris.

he was riding home through the unlit streets of Paris after a rendezvous with Queen Isabella. Suddenly from the dark recesses of doorways the assassins dashed out, grabbed Louis's horse, and shouting "Death to the Duke!" pulled him from his horse. Louis protested, "I am Louis the Duke of Orléans," but they hurled him to the cobblestone street and brutally beat him to death. Though the Duke was thoroughly dead, the killers still feared his sorcery and carefully cut off his left hand to make sure that none of his black magic could escape and cause harm. On hearing the commotion, a cobbler's wife opened her shutters and shrieked, "Murder, murder!" but the assassins had already fled.

So began a royal feud that would widen into civil war. Duke John the Fearless himself soon fell to an avenging assassin's axe. This retaliation had dire consequences. John the Fearless's son, Duke Philip the Good, was not so aptly named; he was elegant, arrogant, and cruel, prone to fits of temper in which his face turned blue with rage. Thirsting to avenge his father's death, he blamed the mad King's son, his cousin Prince Charles, for the murder and declared open civil war against the royal family and all its followers. A bitter struggle between the Royalist party and the Burgundians ensued. A house divided against itself, the kingdom of France seemed on the verge of collapse.

For some time, France's old enemy England had been watching these events unfold from across the channel. With a mad French king and fighting among the royal family, the young English King, Henry V, saw his chance to reach for the French crown. In 1415 he invaded France, renewing a war that had gone on intermittently for almost 100 years, and has earned the name The Hundred Years' War. Though greatly outnumbered, the

English won a resounding victory at the famous battle of Agincourt, killing thousands of French noble knights.

Even worse times were to come for the French. In the year 1420, Duke Philip of Burgundy connived with Queen Isabella in a treacherous plot. Together they persuaded the poor mad King, who hardly knew what he was doing, to sign a treaty with France's archenemy, England! In exchange for military help from the English against Philip's rivals in the civil war, it was agreed that King Henry V of England would marry the French princess and inherit the throne of France. He would be King of both France and England while the rightful heir to the French throne, the only remaining son of the mad King and Isabella, would be disinherited. The Queen, a tool and perhaps a mistress of Duke Philip, did nothing to deny the gossip, spread by the Duke, that her son was illegitimate.

This humiliating treaty, known as the Treaty of Troyes, seemed the last straw in a series of disasters that befell the French. To the French people who loved their King, mad or not, the treaty was a sellout to the enemy. The French national emblem, white lilies on a blue background, was now quartered with the English lions. Many a Frenchman resented the sight of royal banners and shields showing the fierce English lions alongside the pure white lilies of France.

With the Treaty of Troyes, the promise of the French throne, and the alliance with the powerful Duke of Burgundy, the English felt they had all but won the Hundred Years' War. While the English entrenched themselves in Normandy, their ally Duke Philip took over the government of Paris. Soon the Anglo-Burgundians controlled most of the north of France. It looked as though the invaders had come to stay.

The elegant Duke Philip of Burgundy surrounded by his courtiers. Bibliothèque Royale Albert I, Brussels.

Though the English didn't openly say so, what they really wanted was to exploit the rich, fertile lands of France, especially its lush vineyards, which produced the best wines in the world. Campaigning in France became a profitable business for the English. Many an English knight made his fortune there, many an English manor or castle was built with the ransom and loot plucked from victories over the French.

Everywhere people talked of the great misery spreading through France as the English knights plundered the land. Even some French knights sank to ransacking the land, their own land. When formal war was not being fought, soldiers turned into brigands and went on looting sprees, stealing crops and cattle, raping women, then setting fire to villages and manors. Terrorists of their day, they put their captives up for ransom— if payment didn't come quickly, they slit their throats.

The peasants whose farms were destroyed suffered the most while the nobles continued their dissipated lives of worldly pleasure. Despite the war, the royal and ducal courts displayed greater extravagance and luxury than ever. So while the aristocrats played and intrigued, the poor grew more and more wretched.

The Catholic Church (all European Christians were Catholics at that time), so long a source of unity, comfort, and inspiration to the people, had also been corrupted by politics, wealth, and power. One outspoken bishop minced no words in criticism: "Alas, the Church is fallen as low as possible . . . she wallows in the mud of cupidity and debauchery and her avarice chains her to the earth."

There had been a split in the Church known as the "Great Schism," which had recently undermined the prestige of both Church and Pope. Rival popes had been elected, one who lived in France, one in Rome. Though the split had ended in 1417, much harm had been done to the spiritual authority of Church and Pope. But the Church became defensive as critics spoke out; instead of reforming, it stiffened resistance against any new ideas, labeling them heresy. Both Church and nobility were deeply afraid that heresy might lead to revolts among the peasantry and might even threaten the very fabric of society and the unity of the Catholic faith.

The people were losing confidence in both state and Church. Added to the horrors of war, disease and famine stalked the land. Seeing their homes go up in flames, their families die from terrible epidemics like the Black Death that struck again and again, people looked in vain to the Church for help. Victims of the Black Death were covered with swellings, their flesh turned black, and they died within days. Corpses, piled up in city streets, attracted wolves, who feasted on the dead bodies.

Many thought the world was coming to an end. Some thought God was punishing the French people for their sins, others that He had abandoned them. In turn some abandoned God. The most bitter and disillusioned turned to the Devil for help, defying the Church that had failed them. It was believed that the Devil could make one rich, a temptation the most destitute found hard to resist. That strange phenomenon, witchcraft, always ready to emerge in times of crisis, began to surface, touching all classes of society. In the rural countryside ancient beliefs in magic and demons still lingered beneath the mantle of Christianity. The Church grew alarmed; and its own fears and suspicions only increased and helped to spread belief in witchcraft. Churchmen began to suspect witches under every peasant bed just as McCarthyites once saw communists everywhere in our own time. Many innocent peasants were investi-

Dance of Death: A grinning skeleton leading a woman off to hell. Author's collection.

gated for such trivial things as using herbs and spells to cure a sick cow, which was hardly the same as selling one's soul to the Devil. A witch-hunt was in the making.

The miseries and pessimism of daily life show in the art of the times, which reveals a morbid preoccupation with death. Realistic portraits replaced the more idealistic, spiritual art of the earlier Middle Ages. The beauties of paradise were replaced by the horrors of hell. "The Dance of Death," showing skeletons grinning maliciously as they lead the dying off to hell, became a popular theme in works of art.

Though the general misery had little effect on the nobility, Queen Isabella's son, Prince Charles, true heir to the French throne, was having his own troubles. That treacherous treaty with the English, signed by his own mother and the Duke of Burgundy, had disinherited him in favor of the English King. Charles's loyal followers had smuggled him out of Paris when the terrible royal feud began and he was living in exile near the Loire River, surrounded by his Royalist supporters. North of the Loire River was the occupied zone, controlled by English and Burgundians except for a few pockets of resistance.

In 1422, just two years after the treaty, both the mad King Charles of France and King Henry of England died, plunging France into even greater disarray. Henry's infant son was proclaimed king of France and England. His uncle, the Duke of Bedford, would rule as regent until the baby-King came of age. Prince Charles, better known as the Dauphin (a title bestowed on the heir apparent by the province of Dauphiné), now became the focus of resistance against the usurpers and the only hope of restoring the French crown to its lawful dynasty. Though well educated and trained for kingship, Charles lacked confidence and courage. Unable to make up his own mind, he turned to his courtiers or astrologers for advice. Astrology had become fashionable with the nobility, and those who could afford it had their own private seers to consult the stars.

Tensions mounted as rumors spread that English forces were heading toward Charles's domain. In the fall of the year 1428, the English laid siege to the town of Orléans on the Loire River. Orléans was the gateway to the south. Should it be taken, all France would be prey to the foreign enemy and their treacherous allies, the Burgundians. There was much talk but little action. The Dauphin and his supporters began to despair.

It seemed that only a miracle could save them. And a miracle was at hand, from an unlikely source.

1

JOAN AND HER VILLAGE

"Out of the oak forests of Lorraine will come a virgin to save France," ran the age-old prophecy of King Arthur's legendary wizard, Merlin.

On Tuesday, May 10, 1429, a clerk of the Parliament of Paris was busily writing down a report that had just come in from the battlefront. The English had been laying siege to the town of Orléans for nine months and rumors had been flying around that the French were about to surrender. But the clerk was writing something quite different—the French Royalist army had broken the siege of Orléans and the English were in full retreat!

The clerk further reported that the French "had in their company a maid alone, bearing a banner." Fascinated by such an unusual tidbit, he couldn't refrain from drawing his impression of the maid, whom he had never seen, in the margin of his report. Showing a young girl holding a banner and a sword, this tiny sketch is the only one made in her lifetime that has come down to us. What was a teenage girl doing at the forefront of French royal troops in the battle of Orléans? Where had she come from?

This, of course, was Joan of Arc, France's most popular

The clerk's sketch of his idea of Joan in the margin of his report. Archives Nationales, Paris.

heroine and saint. She came from the little village of Domremy, which lies along the Meuse River bordering Lorraine, now the northeastern part of France. The Meuse winds slowly through a valley of fields and meadows, rich with wildflowers. Cattle and sheep graze below gently sloping wooded hills. The early-morning mists hang low over the valley, but when the sun breaks through, all is bathed in warmth and color.

Joan of Arc was born in 1412 in a small stone-and-rubble house next to the village church. Originally the house had

Joan's stone-and-rubble house in Domremy. Now a museum. French Government Tourist Office.

Interior of a peasant house such as Joan's. Author's collection.

three or four small rooms, with a loft above, reached by a ladder. The main room where Joan's mother and father slept was also used for cooking and eating. A drain in the middle of the floor was for slops and led to a ditch below. Water had to be fetched from the village well and what washing was done of the body—usually only hands and face—was in a wooden bucket. Joan and her sister, Catherine, slept in a tiny room to the rear, her three brothers in an adjoining room.

The fact that the house was made of stone and not wood shows that its owners were of some substance and importance. Joan's father, Jacques d'Arc, was one of the leaders of the village. He was not only the collector of taxes for the town's overlord but also head of the village watch, seeing to the safety of the peasants and their livestock in times of enemy raids. At such times of crisis, Joan and her sister and brothers helped their father drive the animals to a refuge, a fortified château on an island in the river.

Joan grew to be a healthy, strong peasant of square build. Her hair was black, her eyes dark brown, and her complexion swarthy. That is all we know of her looks. No one ever called her beautiful—though some remarked on her shapely figure. All were struck by her lovely, feminine voice. Like most peasants, she could neither read nor write and her religious education was simple, learned entirely from her mother. She knew the Lord's Prayer, the Hail Mary, and the Catholic creed. Joan had a cheerful disposition and many friends. She was generous and outgoing, eager to help those in trouble. She willingly gave up her bed to visitors, and once gave it to a sick friend and nursed him back to health. One of her friends teased her for being too pious and told how Joan, out working in the fields, often kneeled to pray when she heard the church bells ringing.

Joan loved the sound of church bells, calling people to prayer at certain times of the day. Whenever the bell ringer forgot his job, Joan became upset. Once she even went to see him. With tears in her eyes—Joan cried easily—she begged him and even bribed him with little cakes not to forget to ring the bells at the regular times: morning, noon, afternoon, and evening.

Church bells had many functions, acting as clocks when they rang to summon people to prayer or as calendars when they summoned villagers to saints' feasts. They were alarms in times of disaster or raids, and when blessed by a priest, they were thought to ward off storms or evil. Villages like Domremy depended on them. In these days of anxiety and fear, Joan found the church bells reassuring, a symbol of order and security.

Named for an early Christian martyr, St. Remi, Domremy today looks much the same as it did in the Middle Ages. Houses with red-tiled roofs, gardens, chicken coops, and livestock in the rear line the town's one central street. The street follows much the same course that Roman legions and, before them, Celts tramped along in centuries past.

Both Celts and Romans left the imprints of their cultures on the countryside. Scattered Roman ruins stirred the imaginations of medieval peasants, who thought them haunted by spirits of the dead, or fancied them as meeting places for fairies and demons. By Joan's time one ancient Roman ruin was known as "the Garden of the Fairies." Though Christianity had replaced the old pagan religions, it hadn't stamped out the nature-oriented beliefs of the peasants. Ancient sacred spots, trees, rocks, and springs continued to be worshipped but under new protectors, the Christian saints. Saints became popular, their miracles even more spectacular than the magic of pagan deities. By Joan's day there were saints for all occasions, saints to protect women in childbirth, saints to cure disease and ward off evil, and saints to protect virginity. Peasants were more apt to pray to saints than to God; saints seemed closer and more human, a little more humble, like peasants themselves. And the saints were all around—in stained-glass windows, in statues, and in church dramas where their lives were acted out. Joan was especially devoted to two virgin saints, St. Catherine and St. Margaret. St. Margaret's statue, at which Joan often prayed, can still be seen in her village church. She also admired the local patron, St. Michael, whose sword gave assurance of protection against evil.

But the saints didn't drive out the nature spirits completely; peasants couldn't shake their old beliefs that good and bad demons still haunted their woodlands and springs. Such was the folk religion of Joan's countryside, a mixture of Christian and pre-Christian beliefs.

In the fifteenth century Joan's village was rocked by intermittent violence and sudden devastating raids of English-Burgundian brigands. It was one of the few pockets of resistance to the encroaching armies of the English and Burgundians. The huge Duchy of Burgundy was not far off, a little to the southwest. Its rich and powerful Duke, Philip the Good, owned vast estates of land in the north and controlled Lorraine, which lay east of the Meuse River. Domremy itself was fiercely loyal to the French Prince Charles but loyalties in the area were divided and feelings ran high. War affected the children too. The youths of Domremy often clashed in local fights with the youths of the pro-Burgundian village of Maxey, just across the river. Joan had seen friends coming back wounded and bleeding.

The English-Burgundian policy was to wear down the French Royalists by plundering the countryside. They burned and destroyed the villages and farms, and often stole the peasants' most precious possession, their cattle.

When Joan was about eleven, her cousin's husband was killed in a Burgundian attack on a nearby village. Joan knew one Burgundian in her neighborhood and remarked that she would like to have seen his head chopped off, "that is, if it were pleasing to God." She was fanatically loyal to the French cause, as were her parents. Two years after her relative was killed, a band of mercenaries, out for loot, descended on Domremy. The church bells rang out the alarm furiously but too late. The brigands managed to steal all the cattle, the farm crops, even household furniture and farm tools. Luckily this time the village was not set on fire and, in answer to an appeal, the local overlord went in hot pursuit, retrieved the cattle, and put the gang leader to death. Such violence, so upsetting to a peaceful farm life, only increased the peasants' bitterness. They had come to hate the Burgundians for their treachery, but they hated the English even more. They despised these overseas invaders as beer-drinking gluttons, and derisively called them "goddons" because of their constant use of "God-damn."

In normal times Joan, like all the village peasants, followed a set routine of farm life, laboring from dawn to dusk, but there were times of fun for young and old alike. From her cottage door Joan could see the oak forest, the Bois Chenu, a little over a mile to the south, and the towering hilltop castle of the village overlords, the Bourlemonts, who owned the forest.

Soldiers raid and loot a village. Author's collection.

Peasants dancing around the Fairies' Tree. Author's collection.

The forest was much larger than it now is—boar and wolves, and some thought werewolves, too, lurked within. In a clearing near this forest stood a huge beech tree, then thought to be three hundred years old. Long venerated, it was called "the Fairies' Tree," and sometimes "the Ladies' Tree." Nearby was a sacred fountain said to have healing powers; mothers often brought sick children here to be cured of the fever. On certain days of the year, especially in the month of May when the renewal of spring was celebrated, villagers gathered at this spot to sing, dance, and picnic. Girls and boys made flower garlands to hang on the tree, reenacting an ancient pagan ritual. Joan had a godmother who claimed she had once seen a fairy there, but Joan doubted it. As for the gossip that witches gathered there on Thursday nights for their meetings, or "sabbats," she scorned such rumors as befitting only those who believed in sorcery. But Joan may have enjoyed the old fairy tale, told by firesides on winter nights, of one lord of Bourlemont who went regularly to the Fairies' Tree to meet a fairy, disguised as a beautiful woman, with whom he fell in love. According to the story, when the lord's wife discovered them, the fairy vanished into thin air.

The Fairies' Tree was also the focus of an ancient pagan fertility rite that had been converted to a Christian ritual. Just before Ascension Day, the local priest, holding a cross, led a procession of villagers carrying banners and ringing bells to ward off evil spirits. They stopped occasionally to bless crops and wells, then wound up by the Fairies' Tree and fountain, where the priest read the Gospel. As in pagan times, this ritual was designed to ensure good harvests and plentiful water. Though the medieval Church tolerated such Christianized pagan rites, Joan knew from her mother that the Church banned belief in all fairies, good or bad. Still, many a farmer thought it wise to put out food at night lest mischievous imps do harm to his crops. Most peasants knew, too, that the wise old women of the village could cure an illness with healing herbs better than a doctor. Such herbs are in vogue again today.

There was great excitement in the village whenever a wandering vendor appeared. His shop, a huge basket strapped to his back, was full of little images of saints, good luck charms, and other trinkets. Sometimes he strummed on his fiddle and sang songs or told tales of chivalry and romance. He always drew a crowd and he usually had news picked up along the way. Joan and other villagers hung on his every word when he reported the latest horrors of war.

One bit of good news reached Domremy in 1425, when Joan was thirteen years old. The little island of Mont-Saint-Michel, protected by France's popular Saint Michael, patron saint of the royal family as well as of Domremy, had staved off an English attack. Might there be some hope of rescuing the kingdom of France after all? Could the terrible English invaders somehow be forced to go back to England? That year there was much talk in the village and in Joan's home of the pitiable plight of France. Joan took all these things to heart.

One day of this same year Joan had an awesome, mystical experience that changed her life. At noon, when the church bells rang out, Joan was alone in her father's garden and seemed to hear a voice coming from the right, from the direction of the village church, and at the same time she saw a bright light. Filled with both fear and elation she told no one of this supernatural experience, not her village priest to whom she often confessed, not even her parents. Only much later, during her trial for witchcraft, did Joan claim that it was the voice of St. Michael she had heard on that day. When asked how she knew it was St. Michael, she said simply, "I believed it quite soon and I had the will to believe it." St. Michael at first only urged her to lead a good life and told her that God would help her. From that point on her revelations became more frequent and more specific.

Skeptics often attribute Joan's revelations to mental illness or hallucinations, but Joan was not at all psychotic. In fact she was a healthy, normal girl, full of good common sense. She was quite unlike the medieval ascetic mystics who, after long fasts, went into trances; nor was she like the educated mystic nuns who had visions of paradise or prophesied doom for unrepentant sinners. Though Joan ate sparingly and drank little wine, she never made a practice of fasting. Her visions were more of this world than of the hereafter, and she made no special claims to supernatural powers. When she was at the peak of her fame, a noble lady remarked how eager people were for Joan's "miraculous" touch. Joan said to her, "Touch them yourself. It will do them just as much good."

But Joan was convinced that her "voices," as her revelations have always been called, came from God. This was not unusual in the Middle Ages, when almost everybody believed in supernatural signs. No one would have doubted that Joan heard voices, especially during that time of crisis when people were looking for just such an inspired visionary to heal their war-torn country. Joan, however, was not yet ready to reveal herself and kept her voices a deep secret.

Some people have thought that Joan's voices were the inner promptings of her conscience. But whether Joan really heard voices or only thought she did doesn't matter. Whatever they were and whatever their source, they were very real to her and gave her extraordinary courage and conviction.

Joan's voices became more frequent at the very time when reports of enemy activity became more alarming. English and Burgundians were planning an all-out attack on the few towns still loyal to the exiled Dauphin Charles, uncrowned King of France. The town of Orléans on the Loire River was a prime target; Vaucouleurs, a few miles north of Domremy, was another.

Joan spent less and less time with her friends as her inner life became more important to her. To the annoyance of her friends and family she often didn't show up for village festivities like the dancing and singing at the Fairies' Tree. Sometimes when her parents thought she was out working in the fields, she went off to one of her favorite haunts, a secluded little chapel in the woods north of her village, to pray before a little wooden statue of the Virgin Mary. In this solitary spot, with only the sound of rustling trees or the song of a bird, she may well have best heard her voices. Later, when on trial,

Joan revealed that two more saints had joined St. Michael to talk to her. These were her adored St. Catherine and St. Margaret, in whom she had often confided. Their courageous lives as virgins inspired Joan to vow to remain a virgin "as long as it was pleasing to God."

Soon the real importance of her messages became clear to her—she had been chosen by God to go to the rescue of Dauphin Charles and the kingdom of France! Joan was quite stunned. How could she, only a poor girl who knew nothing of riding war-horses or making war, undertake such a task! But her secret counsel was giving her more confidence and courage. She began to accept the fact that she had a heroic destiny to fulfill. Her mission, to be sure, was more military and political than spiritual, but it fitted the medieval idea of a God-supported crusade against the wrong of a foreign invasion.

In June 1428, when Joan was sixteen, her village suffered its worst attack. The enemy, preparing to lay siege to Vaucouleurs, was laying waste the neighborhood, plundering and burning nearby villages and farms. Forewarned, all the villagers of Domremy, carrying their possessions, and driving their livestock, fled south to the fortified town of Neufchâteau. Joan and her family stayed with an innkeeper, Madame la Rousse. When Joan was on trial, her judges, trying to smear her reputation, insinuated that Madame la Rousse was a woman of ill repute, that her inn was nothing but a brothel, and that Joan had led an immoral life there. Her accusers cleverly linked this to an incident that occurred soon after her stay at Neufchâteau. Joan was summoned to appear in court in the town of Toul to answer an accusation that she had broken a promise to marry. Joan won the case, proving that she had not given any pledge to marry—after all, Joan planned *never* to marry and had sworn to remain a virgin. But the judges at her later trial for witchcraft, eager to slander her, disregarded her virginity and twisted the facts; they claimed it was the young man in question who wanted to break off the engagement because of Joan's wanton behavior when staying with Madame la Rousse. Little is known about this marriage plan, which must have been arranged by her parents, as was the custom. That Joan refused to go along with it showed a bold independence, if not defiance.

When the villagers returned from Neufchâteau to Domremy they found their little village all but ruined—even the church had been burned. The village set up strict safety rules: No fires were to be lit in homes lest brigands use them to spread arson; no one was to go beyond a barricaded area. One poor farmer, eager to retrieve a plow he had left outside the safety zone, was caught off-limits and made to pay a fine. Added to all this trouble and worry was the disturbing news that the governor of Vaucouleurs was about to surrender his town to the English, and that the English had laid siege to the strategic city of Orléans. Joan's voices became more urgent than ever, now telling her that she should go to Vaucouleurs, get help from the Governor, Robert de Baudricourt, and prepare to go to the rescue of the exiled Dauphin and his besieged town of Orléans. Joan now had a clear, specific mandate.

Though Joan kept her revelations secret, her father may have suspected something. Joan heard from her mother that he had had a terrible dream of Joan joining up with soldiers and going off to war. He had told her brothers to drown her if this turned out to be true and added that if they wouldn't, he would do so himself! Going off with soldiers meant only one thing to her father—that his daughter would be a camp follower, a prostitute. Joan's parents kept a tight rein on her from then on.

As a teenager Joan had become a worry to her parents. Though more pious than ever, Joan was not the meek little girl, not the "goody-goody" she has often been depicted as. Her convictions were too strong for that. Joan's aloofness from friends, her independence, and her refusal to marry naturally upset her parents. She seemed to be defying the conventions of her peasant village. And her parents didn't yet know the worst—that Joan was planning to run away from home. Joan realized that this would not be easy, but she saw no other way. By this time she was so dedicated to her cause that nothing could stop her; she had to find a way to escape soon. It distressed her that she dared not tell her parents of her plans, but she knew they would prevent her from leaving home. Her mission had to come first. Joan later testified, "If I had had a hundred mothers and fathers and if I had been a king's daughter, I would have gone." Her one hope of getaway was through a ruse.

Her first cousin, married to a man named Durand Laxart, was expecting a baby soon. The couple lived conveniently near Vaucouleurs, in the outlying village of Burey. Joan offered to go to Burey to help the young mother. Somehow this was arranged and Durand Laxart came to get her late in December of the year 1428. Joan was wearing the typical peasant girl's outfit, a dark red homespun skirt and bodice. She would not have it for long, and she would never return to her peasant life in Domremy.

The River Meuse. The oak forest in the background. French Government Tourist Office, New York City.

2

❧

THE RUNAWAY

"Go, go, let come what may."

Durand Laxart was fifteen years older than Joan, and she usually called him uncle. They seem to have been fond of each other, and Joan soon confided to him her rather startling plan—to get help to go to the rescue of the Dauphin Charles and have him crowned King. "Was there not a prophecy," she asked her uncle, "that France would be lost by a woman and saved by a virgin?" The "woman" Joan referred to was the hated Queen Isabella, who had disinherited her own son, Prince Charles, and sold out to the enemy. In the fifteenth century, such prophecies were commonplace, and were often used as political propaganda and to stir up enthusiasm for a cause.

Obsessed with her mission, Joan begged Durand to introduce her to the Governor of Vaucouleurs, Robert de Baudricourt, whose help she needed. Joan knew all about Baudricourt, especially since her father had seen him only the year before about some village taxes. She knew that Baudricourt was a royal representative, owing allegiance directly to the exiled Dauphin. She also knew of his loyalty to the French cause and his hatred of the English. Though he had been forced into a temporary truce with the enemy, he had not yet surrendered. Like Orléans and the few other towns loyal to Charles, Vaucouleurs was hanging on by only a thin thread.

No one knows what Durand felt about going along with his young cousin's outlandish ideas or how he thought he could arrange an audience with the great Sire de Baudricourt. But he seems to have been unable to resist Joan's compelling and persuasive personality.

When Joan, accompanied by her "uncle," entered the walled town of Vaucouleurs, she stepped into a new life, soon to broaden into a public career. Though the distance in miles between Domremy and Vaucouleurs was small—only about twelve miles—this town was worlds apart from her farm village. With its many towered thick walls surrounded by a moat, its narrow streets teeming with people, this fortress town must have seemed a metropolis to Joan, whose little village had less than one hundred inhabitants.

Durand had some friends, a wheelwright and his wife, the Le Royers, who agreed to let Joan stay with them. But Durand's next problem was more difficult: How could he, a poor peasant, introduce his insistent young relative to the lord of the town, Sire Robert de Baudricourt, whose imposing castle towered above the city's walls? Perhaps he used the good name of Joan's father, well known to the Governor, to gain an audience. Baudricourt, an aristocrat and a hardened knight, was not too pleased at the prospect of talking to a young peasant girl, especially one claiming she had a mission. Probably she was just another one of those female visionaries of whom there had been so many lately, claiming all sorts of wild things. But for whatever reason, he finally agreed to see her.

Fortified gateway to Vaucouleurs. © Musée Lorrain, Nancy / photo G. Mangin.

Still in her poor peasant dress and accompanied by Durand, Joan walked up the steps to the castle and was ushered into the great hall. This first interview did not go well for Joan. She stepped forth boldly and told Baudricourt that she had been sent to him by her Lord so that the sire would advise the Dauphin Charles that her Lord would send him help before mid-Lent. She said that her Lord wanted Charles to be made king and to recover the kingdom of France. Asked who her Lord was, Joan replied "God." At that Baudricourt exploded in laughter and said to Durand, "Take her home and tell her father to box her ears."

Joan was discouraged but she did not give up. She probably went back to her uncle's home, but soon returned to the Le

Royers in Vaucouleurs, where she stayed several weeks. She became a familiar sight in her red peasant dress as she walked daily through the narrow crowded streets of the lower part of town to the castle chapel on the hill where she had been given permission to pray. Kneeling before the Virgin Mary's statue, she prayed for the success of her mission and a speedy response from the Governor.

People grew curious about this girl from out of town and began to talk to her. One day a young man-at-arms stationed in the town's garrison approached her and said in a friendly way, "My dear, what are you doing here?" Then he asked her, "Must the King be driven out of his kingdom? Will we all have to become English?" This, of course, gave Joan a chance to tell her story. "I have come here," she said, "to speak to Robert de Baudricourt that he might condescend to bring me or have me brought to the King, but he does not take any notice of me or my words; yet before mid-Lent, I must be before the King, even though I were to wear out my legs up to my knees. No one in the world, not kings, nor dukes . . . nor any other can recover the kingdom of France. There is no help but through me. . . . I must go because it is my Lord's will." Asked once more who her Lord was, Joan replied, "God." Unlike Baudricourt, the young man, who was named Jean de Metz, seemed mesmerized and responded enthusiastically. He put his hand in hers to pledge his allegiance and to indicate that he would follow her. He asked her when she would leave. Joan answered, "Better today than tomorrow, better tomorrow than later." Soon Joan was making other converts.

Her popularity in the town may well have been gratifying but Joan was getting more and more frustrated as she waited for the Governor to change his mind and give his permission for her mission. Her hostess, Madame Le Royer, said that Joan was like a pregnant woman impatient for delivery.

Even if Joan couldn't impress Baudricourt, word of her great cause became well known. Eager to believe in miracles in those difficult times, the people began to think there *was* something special about this young girl, that she might indeed have been sent by God to rescue France. They began to talk of her mission as a crusade, and the crusaders' cry "God wills it!" echoed through the streets, as more and more people were captivated by her fervor.

Her faithful friend Jean de Metz, as convinced as she that her great adventure would soon begin, asked if she would leave in the peasant clothes she was wearing. When Joan told him she would willingly put on male clothes, he gave her his servant's shirt and leggings, all too big for her. She must have looked funny, and her other admirers felt she should have a better outfit. They soon provided her with a tunic, long hose, and leather boots. They also bought her a horse. Then she had her hair cut in boyish fashion, short above the ears. Her red dress was cast aside forever.

Without Joan's knowing it, Baudricourt was having second thoughts. He was disturbed by Joan's influence, not only on the townsfolk but also on some of his hard-bitten soldiers. He dispatched a royal messenger to his overlord, Charles, asking whether the Dauphin would give an audience to a peasant girl who said that God had commanded her to come to his rescue.

Meanwhile Joan received a strange invitation. By now her fame had spread beyond the walls of Vaucouleurs, and the Duke of Lorraine requested that she come to see him. It seems odd that Joan would go to Lorraine, known to be pro-Burgundian, but a request from so important a person was tantamount to a command. Besides, Joan may have seen this as a chance to make another convert. Her horizons were expanding.

The Duke of Lorraine, who was old and sick, lived in great opulence in a palace even grander than the castle at Vaucouleurs. He was not at all interested in Joan's mission. What he was concerned about was his health, and he hoped that Joan's reputation as a girl with supernatural powers meant that she was one of those village "wise women" who could cure people. Already myths about Joan as a miracle worker were in the making. But Joan told him frankly that she knew nothing about the arts of healing, and that his health might improve only if he behaved better, gave up his mistress, and went back to his good spouse—not exactly what the Duke wanted to hear. Then Joan boldly told him that she needed to go to Chinon to find Charles the Dauphin, and asked him to lend her some men-at-arms. Though she had not healed the Duke and he didn't respond to her request, he was impressed enough to give her a few gold pieces and a black horse.

Back in Vaucouleurs Joan was overjoyed to find that Baudricourt had changed his mind. No one knows just what swayed the tough, cynical Governor to lend support to the peasant girl he had at first rejected. Perhaps he dared not go against the enthusiasm she had aroused among both the townsfolk and his own soldiers. She might be crazy but what could he lose by giving her a chance?

A later tale explained his turnabout more dramatically. It was said Joan had startled the Governor by telling him that the French had just, that very day, been defeated by the English in a battle near Orléans. Baudricourt soon found out that this was true and was amazed. How could Joan have known unless she had the telepathic powers of a clairvoyant? Possibly she did—or maybe the entire tale was an invention, made up after the fact. At any rate a message from the Dauphin agreeing to give audience to the peasant maid pushed Baudricourt to his decision. If his overlord, the Dauphin, was willing to see the girl, he could hardly refuse to help her on her way.

Still, there was one more stumbling block. Before he gave Joan his final permission, Baudricourt took the precaution of having her exorcized. He believed, as did everyone in those days, that demons could disguise themselves as angels or saints, and that Joan might be possessed and guided by evil instead of good spirits. One day, accompanied by a priest, he appeared at the home of the Le Royers, where Joan was staying. To have the Governor call on this simple family in the lower part of town was a surprise and a most unusual honor. The priest, whom Joan already knew, was dressed in his clerical garb. Making the sign of the cross and pronouncing the formula of exorcism, he told Joan that if there was any evil in her, it must depart, and that if her spirit was good, it should come forth. Joan stepped forward and knelt before the priest but rebuked him, saying he had not acted properly since he had heard her in confession and knew she had no evil spirit.

Now Baudricourt was satisfied and gave the longed-for permission. He also gave Joan a sword and another horse. (The number of horses Joan managed to acquire in her short life is quite staggering!) Joan's small escort consisted of Jean de Metz, his squire, an archer, the royal messenger, and three servants.

Baudricourt made them swear to protect Joan and guide her safely to the Dauphin. Late in February 1429, at the beginning of Lent, the little group assembled at the town's western gate, known as the Gate of France. Crowds of people were there to see them off. Joan, armed only with her sword, was dressed in a black belted tunic under a coarse linen cape. Over her long brown hose were tightly laced leggings. She had spurs on her high leather boots and she wore a black cap. She was only seventeen, her companions not much older. As the group rode through the gate, Baudricourt called out to them, "Go, go, let come what may."

3

❧

CHINON

"Take me to Orléans and I will give you the signs for which I was sent."

The three-hundred-fifty-mile trip to the great castle of Chinon where Charles lived was not easy in mid-February. Winter rains had flooded the many rivers they had to cross and much of the way was through enemy territory in the duchy of Burgundy. Joan was asked if she was not afraid. According to one of her friends, Joan replied that "she was not, because the path was open to her. If there were warriors on the way, she had God, her Lord, who would clear the road for her to go to the Dauphin and that she was born to do this." Even so they took the precaution of traveling mostly at night and circling around larger towns. They passed many abandoned villages, ruined by recent warring marauders. Sometimes they slept in deserted barns but more often on the cold, damp ground. Joan, fully clothed, slept beside her faithful Jean de Metz and his squire. These young men later confessed that at first they were tempted to make sexual advances but quickly realized that Joan was not that sort of girl. Something about her stopped them. Joan knew the value of her virginity and guarded it well. If Joan ever had any interest in sex or romance, she had to suppress it in order to fulfill her mission as the virgin savior of France.

Others of her escorts had wondered at first if Joan was completely sane to be undertaking this strange adventure. But Joan's courage, her obvious sincerity, and her will to go on, no matter what obstacles confronted them, soon convinced the doubters. It was not long before the whole group was eager and willing to do almost everything she asked. When their spirits flagged, she was able to raise them, telling her companions they should not be afraid, emphasizing again that she had been commissioned by God "to go to war to deliver the kingdom of France."

Whenever Joan saw a church looming up, she wanted to stop to hear mass, but that was one thing her escorts feared to let her do, lest the group be recognized or ambushed by the enemy. However, as they approached the Loire River, they took a chance and, disguising themselves as merchants, went into the large cathedral at Auxerre. Fortunately no harm befell them.

Once across the Loire River they were at last in land belonging to Charles. In the little town of Fierbois they were able to relax for three days. This would be their last stop before reaching their final destination of Chinon, where they would find the exiled Dauphin and his royal court. Joan dictated a letter to Charles announcing her impending arrival, stating that she had traveled one hundred fifty leagues to come to his aid. Then she went to a chapel dedicated to St. Catherine, a favorite pilgrimage center for released prisoners of war. Rusty old swords, shields, and armor hung on the wall, votive offerings to the saint. Here Joan spent the better part of two days, hearing

Sketch of Chinon Castle, now in ruins. Joan was lodged in the tower at extreme left. By Turner Brooks.

mass and praying before the statue of her beloved St. Catherine.

On the third day Joan received an answer from Charles's council, inviting her to proceed to the royal court in Chinon. As they approached the town, they could see its imposing thick-walled castle sprawled on the crest of a hill high above the Vienne River.

After getting settled in the town of Chinon along the river's edge, Joan, with her faithful knight Jean de Metz, rode up the winding road to the castle. As she was crossing the drawbridge, a rude guard called out, "Isn't that the Maid?" and with a coarse oath added that if he had her for the night, she would no longer be a maiden. It is said that he fell into the moat and drowned.

As at Vaucouleurs, Joan was forced to wait for some time before being allowed an audience with the Dauphin. Though she protested that she wanted to speak immediately and directly to him, she first had to be tested by his council, one of the many tests and interviews that Joan would be subjected to in her short life. After two days of questioning, the council agreed that the Maid spoke well. They were impressed with what seemed her miraculous journey through enemy territory and across swollen rivers without mishap. Finally they were ready to grant her an audience with the Dauphin.

Today only the ruins of the impressive castle of Chinon, long a favorite of French kings, remain. Its great hall is roofless now, but one can feel its ancient grandeur in the huge hollow space between its thick walls. When Joan entered the hall it was dark, save for the flickering of torches, the glint of knights' armor (some three hundred knights were on hand), and the sparkle of courtiers' gilded, jeweled robes. If dazzled, Joan didn't show it but made straight for the Dauphin. Though she had never seen Charles before, she immediately singled him out and knelt before him saying, "Most noble Dauphin, I have come and am sent by God to bring aid to you and your kingdom." She also told Charles that she would last but a little longer than a year and that there was much work to be done in that short time.

The contrast between the confident, inspired young peasant girl in simple male dress and the anxious, uncertain Dauphin Charles smothered in velvet and ermine was indeed dramatic. Much has been made of this scene, including a legend that Charles tried to trick Joan by disguising himself and hiding in the crowd. That Joan knew Charles immediately seemed a miracle to many. Yet it is likely that Joan, whose village was so dedicated to the Dauphin, would have heard him described or seen his likeness on coins or banners. This "noble" Dauphin, whom Joan so admired and wanted to help, lacked kingly bearing. His body was weak, his physique puny, his legs spindly. He had a long bulbous nose and his droopy, listless eyes gave him a sort of vacant look. Unlike Joan, he was plagued by fears. Afraid to cross bridges lest they collapse, he also shied away from strangers and large gatherings, aware of the danger of assassination in crowds. But Joan was not in the least bothered by his looks or weaknesses. To her he was the personification of kingship, a prince who had been maligned and unfairly disinherited by the queen mother, the English, and the Burgundians. Joan was determined to have him properly crowned after she had helped defeat the English in Orléans.

Joan remained devoted to Charles as long as she lived. She also may have been more perceptive than some historians who have overlooked Charles's latent abilities. Despite his physical weaknesses and his cautious and secretive nature, he was no fool. Later in his reign, after Joan's death, he proved to be the leader France needed. Unfortunately, when Joan met him, he was the tool of greedy, malicious advisors. Joan was too naive to realize the corrupt and unsavory quality of many of Charles's courtiers.

Joan was soon moved to one of the castle's towers, the Tour de Coudray, and given a page to attend her. Her life was changing rapidly.

The day after her audience with the Dauphin, one of his royal kinsmen, the dashing young Duke of Alençon, arrived. He was curious to meet this Maid who seemed to have appeared out of nowhere claiming that she could help Charles drive the English out of France. He was immediately captivated by Joan. She greeted him warmly, saying, "You are very welcome. The more of the royal blood of France that are gathered together, the better." Alençon typified to Joan the perfect chivalric knight.

Portrait of the sad-eyed Dauphin Charles. By Fouquet. The Louvre, Paris, Cliché des Musées Nationaux — Paris.

In turn he was impressed with Joan as he watched her practice tilting in the castle courtyard. Bracing a lance she would gallop toward a target and try to hit it squarely. Alençon couldn't resist giving her still another horse.

Though Charles and all who had met her were greatly impressed with Joan, they felt she should be questioned by a group of churchmen to find out if they really should trust this ignorant peasant girl. So Charles and his entire court moved with Joan to Poitiers, where his government advisors, mostly men of the church under the leadership of the eminent Archbishop of Reims, were gathered. Joan was examined almost every day for three weeks, by relays of learned churchmen.

The record of this examination has been lost, but a few of the exchanges have survived. Joan's opening remark was defensive: "I suppose that you have come to question me. But I do not know 'A' from 'B'." One churchman confronted her with the statement, "You have said that a voice told you that God

Practicing tilting at the "quintain," an armed wooden dummy suspended on a pole. If the dummy's shield was not hit squarely, the dummy swung around and whacked the rider with its club. Bibliothèque Royale Albert I, Brussels.

wishes to deliver the people of France from their present calamity. If He wants to deliver them, it is not necessary to send soldiers." Joan parried, "In the name of God, the soldiers will fight and God will deliver them." Joan resented this prying into her private supernatural experiences, which she had not discussed with anyone except, perhaps, Charles. When asked by another churchman, who had a thick provincial accent, what dialect her voice used, Joan impudently answered, "Better than yours." Asked if she believed in God, Joan indignantly snapped back, "Better than you do." Good manners were not part of Joan's peasant upbringing. When she was told that Charles and his council needed some proof or sign from her that God really had sent her, she retorted, "In the name of God, I did not come here to give signs; but take me to Orléans and I will show you the signs for which I was sent."

She was questioned about her male clothes and reminded that the Bible said it was a sin for a woman to dress as a man. But her questioners didn't press this and apparently agreed that it was the only sensible solution for a girl planning to lead soldiers to battle. When asked why she called Charles "Dauphin" instead of "King"—his courtiers already considered him to be King—Joan replied that she could not call him King until he was properly crowned and anointed with holy oil.

While in Poitiers, Joan was subjected to a physical examination to determine whether she was indeed a virgin. The issue of Joan's virginity was as important to her contemporaries as it was to her. Great value was attached to virginity then—it had an aura of magic about it.

In those days everyone believed that a witch could not be a virgin because her pact with the Devil implied sexual relations with him, whereas a virgin could not be contaminated by the Devil. If it turned out that Joan was not a virgin, she would be proved a liar and perhaps even a tool of the Devil—in other words, she might be a witch. But if she was proved to be a virgin, Joan's examiners would be more likely to believe that she was sent by God, in which case she would be thought capable of all sorts of miracles.

She proved to be a virgin, and the churchmen found nothing but good in her testimony. They advised Charles to take up her challenge since she undoubtedly was ordered by God to rescue France. Though not fully in charge of French troops, Joan was to help lead them to Orléans, an unusual honor for a woman, and one who was only a peasant at that.

In her impatience to be off to Orléans, Joan dictated a letter to the English telling them to surrender, to "the Maid sent by God, the keys of all the good towns which you have taken and violated in France." She told them to raise the siege of Orléans and go home to England or be ready to suffer great injury, and she reminded them that Charles was the true heir to the kingship of France. If they would agree to make peace she would willingly accept it, but if not, they must be prepared for great harm. There was no response— the English did not even return Joan's messenger—and no one knows what the English thought of this bold letter from a peasant girl. They probably took it as a joke.

Back near Chinon, in the town of Tours, Joan waited while armor was made especially for her. Like the extravagant styles of the day—men wore fur-trimmed velvets and sleeves puffed out like balloons, while women flaunted high, cone-shaped hats

The latest style in women's hats, which were getting bigger and bigger. Fifteenth-century manuscript painting. Bibliothèque Nationale, Paris.

with decorative appendages that projected so far the wearers had to duck and walk sideways to get through doors—armor had become ornate and complicated. Joan's was in the latest style with overlapping steel plates and movable plates for knee, elbow, and shoulder joints. Joan's helmet had a visor that could be lowered to protect her face. Her thighs were protected by a steel skirt, split in the center for riding a horse. Like the shoes of the day, Joan's boots, with tiny overlapping pieces of steel sewed to leather, were elongated to an unwieldy point.

In full armor, Joan was covered from head to toe. Plate armor was far more protective against arrows, crossbow bolts, or sword slashes than chain mail, but it was so heavy—often weighing sixty pounds—that a knight had to be helped onto his horse. Over her armor Joan wore a cloak of gold cloth. That Joan was pleased with this elegant attire, a far cry from the peasant dress she had discarded only five months before, seems quite natural, but her enemies later accused her of excessive love of finery.

Two battle standards, one small and one large, were specially crafted for Joan. On Joan's personal banner Jesus and two angels were painted on white silk. The other one, her company's standard, had an Annunciation scene. Joan was very proud of these standards and preferred them to her sword. She had a feeling that her personal standard kept her from killing, and it is a fact that Joan never did kill anyone even in the thick of battle.

Then there is Joan's sword, whose mysterious discovery has never been explained and is considered to be one of her miracles. Apparently Joan sent for a certain sword she thought was buried near the altar in St. Catherine's Chapel at Fierbois, where she had stayed en route to Chinon. "It was not very deep in the earth," she said. "It was, as I think, behind the altar, but I am not certain whether it was in front or behind it." In the chivalric tradition of King Arthur and his famous sword, Excalibur, the sword was miraculously found in the chapel. Was this clairvoyance or had she glimpsed the sword among the other old and rusty ones when she was praying in the chapel? In any case this sword was precious to Joan because of its connection with her beloved St. Catherine. Many people thought of it as a magic sword. Its rust fell away easily upon rubbing, revealing five crosses on its blade. Two sheaths, one of crimson velvet, the other of gold cloth, were presented to Joan, but she preferred a more practical one of strong leather.

The army headed out to Blois, halfway to Orléans, to join the reinforcements being assembled to go to the aid of the besieged. By now Joan had acquired two squires, two pages, two heralds (for carrying messages), and her own chaplain. Two of Joan's brothers, Jean and Pierre, had also joined her. These were the same brothers who had been told by their father to drown Joan rather than let her go off with soldiers. They were likely the ones who told Joan that her parents nearly went out of their minds when they first found out that she had joined the French army. By now the whole family may have felt differently.

In addition to Alençon, several other well-known knights had joined the group. Even the battle-scarred knight La Hire, who ordinarily would have scorned the peasant maid, fell under her spell. More of a bandit than a perfect chivalric knight, La Hire was famous for his dreadful oaths and a prayer he uttered: "God, I pray You that You will do for La Hire what You would wish La Hire to do for You, if La Hire were God and You were La Hire." When not in armor, he dressed in showy clothes, strutting around in a scarlet cloak sewed all over with little tinkling silver bells. Joan managed to keep him from swearing; at least he never did so in front of her. He became as loyal to her as Alençon was. Another tough warrior, Gilles de Rais, behaved himself while under Joan's influence but after her death sank to the life of a hardened criminal and was believed to be the model for the terrible murderer Bluebeard. That Joan could keep such men in line was indeed miraculous.

Joan directed her chaplain to see that the soldiers went to confession before setting off for battle. With Joan, her chaplain, and other priests in the lead, the knights started east singing "Veni Creator Spiritus." For Joan, leading an army of three to four thousand strong, this was the start of a holy war.

4

THE BATTLE OF ORLÉANS

"It's all yours. Go in!"

When Joan left Blois on April 27, 1429, the town of Orléans had been under siege for almost seven months. Both sides were war-weary and discouraged by the long impasse. The English had not been able to breach the formidable, thirty-foot-high walls. Though they had managed to almost encircle Orléans with forts, one gate, the Burgundy Gate on the east side of the town, remained open for inhabitants to come and go, and for food and supplies to be brought in. But now that opening was threatened too; the English had taken and fortified an old church, St. Loup, only a little over a mile east of this gate. From here they planned to capture and seal off this last entry to the city, and then to starve the French into surrender. The English were waiting for reinforcements before they closed in on the well-guarded walls. It was just a matter of time.

Orléans lies along the north bank of the Loire River. At the time of the siege, its main gate opened onto a stone bridge that spanned the river to the south shore. The southern end of the bridge was defended by massive twin towers, known as

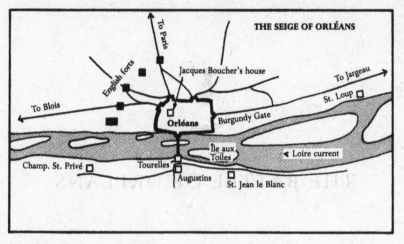

Plan of Orléans, showing English forts, the Burgundy Gate, the Augustins, and the Tourelles. From Francis Gies's Joan of Arc.

the Tourelles. Early in the siege, the English had captured this strategic area and had made it almost impregnable by adding outworks of ditches and palisades along the south shore. This had been a great coup for the English, who not only controlled the main access to the city but now had a foothold in the area south of the Loire River, in the royal land belonging to Charles. In retaliation the French had destroyed two arches of the bridge, leaving an impassable gap just north of the Tourelles that prevented the enemy from storming the city from the bridge. The English blockade of the city, though incomplete, meant that any French relief forces coming from the west would have to make a wide detour around the English forts to get to the one open gate.

Count Dunois, the Bastard of Orléans, was the town's most ardent defender. Though many had deserted, he had remained loyal through the long, discouraging siege. The illegitimate son of the murdered Duke Louis of Orléans, he was usually called the Bastard, a term which then implied no shame, especially when one was of royal blood. He was a courteous, chivalric knight, staunch in his loyalty to his overlord and cousin, the Dauphin.

The French had considered the attack on Orléans a breach of chivalry since its rightful Duke was being held prisoner in the Tower of London and was not on hand to defend his own town. Even some of the English had worried about this unethical conduct but not enough to stop the more eager warmongers. When the greatest of the English knights, the Earl of Salisbury, was killed by a huge cannonball that sheared off half his face, the French felt that God was punishing the English for their unchivalrous conduct.

Though much talked about, chivalry was on the wane. Warfare was slowly changing, and a new weapon, the cannon, would eventually make knightly deeds of prowess obsolete. In this siege, the cannon was still in a trial stage and was used along with older, more tried weapons and tactics. Primitive, inaccurate, and unwieldy, cannons were difficult to load and sometimes backfired, killing the bombadier rather than the enemy. Small cannons, or culverins, which shot lead balls, were more accurate and easier to handle, but of no use in attacking a thick-walled town. The English did once manage to shoot a huge stone cannonball over the walls. It burst through the roof of a tavern, landing in the center of a table where men were drinking, but killed no one.

The French clung to an old but dependable system to detect whether the enemy was "mining" (digging under) its walls. They placed buckets of water at intervals on top of the ramparts. If the water ruffled, they would know a mining operation was going on and could rush to the spot. Women did their part by carrying buckets of boiling oil and hot ashes, and supplies

Siege of Orléans, showing crude cannon. Miniature painting from Les Vigiles du Roi Charles VII. Bibliothèque Nationale, Paris.

of caltrops (lethal little iron balls with spikes) to the soldiers manning the walls, who would then hurl them down on any attackers who attempted to climb up scaling ladders.

During the long siege there had actually been some moments of chivalry. Once, two French knights challenged two English to a joust outside the city walls. Both besieged and besiegers amicably watched the contest as though they were attending their favorite spectator sport. During a truce on Christmas Day the English sent the French a present of figs. The courteous Lord Dunois responded by sending a fur coat to the English commander and lending musicians to the enemy to liven up the holiday. French minstrels sang and played on trumpets and clarions, "making much melody for quite a long time." But as soon as the truce ended, the musicians returned to Orléans and attacks began again.

Just before Joan had left Vaucouleurs for Chinon, the French had suffered their humiliating defeat at the "Battle of the Herrings" (the defeat Joan supposedly had revealed to Baudricourt) when they failed to stop reinforcements from getting through to the English forts surrounding Orléans. Since then morale had sunk lower and lower within the town. Many of its leaders had left, thinking the cause hopeless. The English were now confident that starvation would force the French to surrender any day. Only trickles of food were getting through to the 20,000 inhabitants of Orléans. In their despair, the people were losing their will to resist, not knowing where to turn for help, "unless it be to God."

Then in late February 1429, rumors began to circulate of a virgin savior coming from Lorraine. Despite the secrecy that Joan and her small escort had tried to maintain on their trip from Vaucouleurs to Chinon, peddlers and pilgrims along the highways were spreading strange tales that a young Maid, dressed as a boy, astride a war-horse and accompanied by a few men-at-arms, had been seen in the area. Rumors spread so fast in Orléans that Count Dunois sent messengers to Chinon to find out what these tales could mean. Curiosity and excitement mounted in the next weeks. Finally news came that she who called herself Joan the Maid was indeed on her way to Orléans. Astride a white horse and clad in knight's armor, she was surrounded by priests and followed by men-at-arms, wagonloads of supplies, and cattle, sheep, and pigs. The townsfolk took new hope. No one was more eager to meet the young girl than Count Dunois, who had heard of her dramatic meeting with the Dauphin.

Joan and her companions slept in the open fields on their way from Blois to Orléans. Though Joan found her new armor

Count Dunois, the Bastard of Orléans. **Culver Pictures.**

uncomfortable to sleep in, she did not complain. But when the army stopped on the south shore of the Loire River far beyond and east of Orléans, she had plenty of complaints. Joan had expected to go straight to Orléans, hoping to confront the English right away. No one had explained to her that, coming from Blois, they would find the northern bank blocked by English fortifications. Joan could see Orléans across the Loire—yet here they were on the wrong side of the river and far beyond the town they had come to rescue. Joan obviously didn't know the geography of the area nor the layout of the English blockade. She was hurt and angry that no one had explained the situation to her. But her more experienced companions, knowing they were hampered by slow-moving wagons and animals, had chosen the safest approach. Avoiding the heavily fortified enemy zone north of the Loire, they had come along the safer area south of the river. Joan's dreams of an immediate battle with the enemy seemed to be thwarted, and she felt she couldn't stand any more waiting.

Count Dunois had left Orléans by the Burgundy Gate and crossed the river to meet Joan. When he appeared to greet the young Maid she accosted him. "Are you the Bastard of Orléans?" she asked. Dunois, who had so looked forward to this meeting, politely replied, "I am so and I rejoice in your coming." He must have been startled at Joan's angry next question. "Did you give the order that I should come here to this side of the river, instead of going straight to where the English are?" Dunois replied that he and others wiser than he advised this as the safest and best way, to which Joan retorted, "In God's name, the counsel of God is safer and wiser than yours. You thought you had deceived me but you have deceived yourself, for I bring you better help than any knight or city, the help of the King of Heaven." Dunois quickly realized that this charismatic young girl had a mind of her own.

And now for the first time Joan learned of her commanders' strategy. There was to be no attack on the English until the French got the much-needed provisions safely into Orléans. She could see barges and boats lined up along the riverbank, waiting to be loaded with the food, cattle, and artillery her army had brought. The plan was to sail them across the river to the one free zone and enter Orléans through the Burgundy Gate. But frustration set in as a contrary wind and current made this plan unworkable. Joan, having calmed down from her disappointment, was the one who now advised patience, promising all would be well soon. Sure enough, within a short time the wind shifted, the current slowed, and the convoy crossed the river without a hitch! Dunois and the other knights proclaimed this nothing short of a miracle, and proof that Joan was indeed sent by God. Joan too may have thought this was God's doing, but as a weatherwise farm girl she may instinctively have known that the wind would shift at this late hour of the day. Perhaps it was more miraculous that they were not attacked by the English while waiting outside Orléans for nightfall. Dunois seemed to think entering under cover of darkness would avoid confusion and the press of crowds eager to see the maid.

At eight o'clock on the evening of April 29, Joan rode through the Burgundy Gate. She was fully armed, astride a white horse, her standard raised on high; she was accompanied by Count Dunois and other prominent knights. Despite the dark, the

Joan, in full armor, rides into Orléans on her white horse. Sixteenth-century miniature painting. Cl. Ch. Hémon, Musées Départementaux de Loire-Atlantique, Musée Dobrée, Nantes.

townspeople came out in droves. Carrying torches, they crowded around her, jostling each other to get close enough to touch her. Suddenly sparks from a nearby torch set her standard afire, but Joan quickly spurred her horse, then deftly turned it and extinguished the fire, much to the marvel of all. From now on everything Joan did seemed to have a touch of magic. Legends about her were already in the making. To the joyful cheers of the citizens, she rode over the cobbled streets to the home of the town treasurer, where she and her brothers were to stay.

The good magic that the French saw in Joan was nothing but black magic to the English. Joan, who had had no reply to her letter to the English, sent a second letter, addressed to the English commander, Lord Talbot. She advised him to give up the siege and go back to England or she would force him to do so. She also demanded the return of the herald who had delivered Joan's first message. The English replied rudely that they would burn her when they got hold of her, and that she was nothing but a cowgirl who should go back to tending her animals. Incensed at this, Joan now replied in person. She rode out the south gate on horseback, going as far as she could on the broken stone bridge, and called across the gap to the English in the Tourelles demanding that they surrender in the name of God. The English again replied with curses, asking if Joan expected them to surrender to a peasant girl dressed like a man. They referred to her French escorts as "faithless pimps."

Since her words had no effect on the English, Joan said it was time for a confrontation, but again she had to be patient. Count Dunois felt he needed still more men before attacking the English and went off to Blois to recruit them. He returned three days later, on May 4, with the relieving army—but also with the bad news that an English captain, Sir John Fastolf, was on his way with reinforcements. To Joan, so eager to come to grips with the enemy, this was welcome news. "Bastard, Bastard," she said, "in God's name, I command that, as soon as you hear of the arrival of Fastolf, you will let me know, for if he gets through without my knowing it, I promise I will have your head cut off." Dunois took this with a smile and promised he would let her know.

That same day, Joan was just starting an afternoon rest, when suddenly she sprang up, waking her squire, Jean de Metz. "In God's name, my counsel has told me I must attack the English." She wasn't sure where she should go, but quickly arming, she called for her horse and spurred it toward the Burgundy Gate. She heard someone say that the enemy was doing great harm to the French, and indeed Joan could see Frenchmen running back to the city, some wounded and bleeding.

Without alerting Joan, Dunois had launched an attack on the English fortifications at St. Loup, not quite two miles east of the city. The French were getting the worst of it and were in full retreat when Joan appeared. Seeing her with her white standard raised on high, the French gave a cheer, turned back to the assault, and pressed on with such force that the English suddenly yielded. St. Loup was taken, and the palisades surrounding it were burned to the ground. One hundred fourteen English lay dead, and forty were taken prisoner. Though not a big battle, this was an important victory. It was the first time in this long siege that the French had captured an English fort. Had the French lost, the English surely would have gone on to capture the Burgundy Gate and to seal off Orléans completely.

This was also Joan's first real taste of battle, and the sight of so much blood and so many corpses deeply upset her.

The next day was Ascension Day. Joan decreed that there would be no fighting on this sacred day and urged all to go to confession. Though Joan was never given real military command, those who were in charge recognized her psychological and moral leadership. She somehow managed to make the hard-bitten knights go to confession and refrain from swearing and immoral conduct. She also kept the soldiers from plundering St. Loup, which they normally would have done. Joan's magnetic charm seemed to prevail even in the heat of battle. Most important, she had raised the flagging spirits of the French and spurred them on to victory.

The next time that Lord Dunois called a council of war he included Joan. Feeling more confident, the French decided to launch an attack on the Tourelles and other fortifications near the south end of the bridge over the Loire. After this council, Joan sent a third and final summons to the English to go back to England or suffer the consequences. Since the enemy had kept her earlier messengers hostage, she attached this letter to an arrow, which an archer shot across the broken bridge span to the English. More derisive insults came back. "Here's news from the French strumpet"—at which Joan broke into angry tears.

Early the next morning Joan, Dunois, and other knights leading the French troops forded a shallow part of the river to a small island. From there they crossed to the south shore on a floating bridge of barges. Between them and their main objective, the impregnable Tourelles, was a ruined old Augustinian monastery that the English had fortified. An advance French scouting party set off to reconnoiter the outworks of

The Tourelles at the south end of the bridge to Orléans, scene of Joan's great victory that changed the course of the war. By Turner Brooks.

the monastery only to be confronted by swarms of English charging out. Terrified, the French scouts started to retreat. But Joan rode into the melee, shouting, "Let us go boldly in the name of the Lord." This was enough to rally the French, who turned and charged forward. Getting through the outer palisades, they were confronted by a giant Englishman who was skillfully blocking the main entrance to the monastery, repelling every assault. Suddenly a crackshot gunner, a soldier from Lorraine, took aim and fired his culverin, the small hand cannon, with such rare accuracy that the huge Englishman toppled over. After a brief, furious, hand-to-hand battle, the English fled by a back gate to the safety of the Tourelles.

Darkness was falling, and Joan was persuaded to return to the town of Orléans for the night. As she was eating supper, someone came to tell her that it had been decided in council that they didn't have enough men to attack the Tourelles, that they would have to wait for still more recruits. Joan replied, "You have been in your council and I in mine; and believe me, the council of the Lord will be carried out and will prevail and your council will perish." She told her chaplain to wake her early the next day, that she would have much to do. She added that she knew she would be wounded in the forthcoming fray. Once, when someone had remarked that Joan was not afraid to go into battle because she knew she was protected by God, she replied that she was no safer than anyone else. And now she seemed to know in advance that this was true.

Early the next morning Joan was offered a trout for breakfast but she said, "Keep it until tonight, and I'll bring you back a goddon . . . and I will come back by the bridge," implying she would capture the Tourelles. As she started out of the Burgundy Gate, the town bailiff tried to stop her, saying that no one was to leave the town that day. "Like it or not," said Joan, "the soldiers will go out and they will win as they have won before." The bailiff was helpless against the surging crowd of townspeople and militia, all eager to follow Joan out the gate. After crossing the river, Joan was soon joined by Dunois and the main army.

The Tourelles, manned by about six hundred English soldiers, was much more of a challenge than the old monastery fort. The English had built formidable outworks of deep ditches and massive walls to obstruct any approach to the towers from the south shore of the Loire. Should these be taken, the English could always retreat over the drawbridge between the outworks and the Tourelles.

The attack started at dawn, the French scrambling into ditches and up ramparts. Whenever the French tried to scale the walls, they were showered with arrows, missiles, and cannonballs; if any reached the top, their heads were bashed with maces. Joan wore no helmet that day—to keep up the fighting spirit she wanted to be clearly seen. In the early afternoon she was about to step onto a scaling ladder when her prediction came true. She was hit by an arrow that pierced her exposed neck and came out her back, above her shoulder blade. Crying out with pain and almost fainting, she was carried to a meadow, where someone cut off the arrow tip; but Joan pulled out the shaft herself. When soldiers offered to heal her with charms, she refused, scorning magic and allowing only oil and lard to be applied to her wound. Her friends tended and comforted her and persuaded her to rest awhile. But late in the day she insisted upon mounting her horse and returning to the battle.

As dusk set in, all were exhausted. They had been fighting for thirteen hours and still the towers had not been captured. Dunois was about to sound a retreat but Joan wouldn't hear of it. She begged him to wait, let the troops eat and refresh themselves, and then renew the assault. She added that the Tourelles and the ramparts would soon be taken, that the English were weakening. While the soldiers relaxed, Joan went off by herself to a nearby vineyard to pray for a few minutes. Then, seizing her standard, she rode back to join the renewed attack, heading down into a ditch, below a rampart. According to one account, she said to her page, "Watch for the moment when the tip of my standard touches the rampart." When her page shouted, "Joan, the tip is touching!" she cried, "It's all yours. Go in!"

And now the French closed in from all sides. Help came unexpectedly from the north, where an extraordinary operation had been going on. Some of the town's citizens had been inspired to attempt what seemed an impossible feat. Carpenters with ladders, boards, gutters torn from houses—anything they could use—had been working furiously to build a makeshift wooden walkway to span the gap in the stone bridge to the northern walls of the Tourelles. Hoisted up by ropes and pulleys, the walkway finally rested on the tower wall. As the French soldiers were pouring into the southern fortifications, some of the militia from Orléans were creeping up the precarious wooden bridge in single file, high above the river. The English, sure they were protected against attacks from the north, began to panic as they saw themselves besieged from both north and south at once. As they started to retreat to the drawbridge from the French onslaught of their southern outworks, they met a worse disaster. The French had set fire to a barge loaded with oil-soaked rags, pitch, and bundles of sticks below the drawbridge. The wooden bridge burst into flames and suddenly gave way as the English knights stampeded across. Screaming, they plunged headlong into the river; the weight of their armor dragged them to the bottom. All were drowned, including their commander. Though Joan wept at this ghastly sight, some more worldly Frenchmen merely lamented that so many English nobles worth good ransoms had perished.

As Joan, Dunois, and the victorious French returned to Orléans, flickering fires from the burning Tourelles cast an eerie reflection in the waters of the Loire. In the town, church bells pealed out and the people, wild with joy and thanksgiving, sang "Te Deum Laudamus." Joan was escorted to her lodging to have her wound dressed and to eat her first meal of the day—some bread dipped in a mixture of wine and water; the fish she had promised to eat later was either forgotten or eaten by someone else.

The dramatic change in the course of the war seemed miraculous to the English as well as to the French. To the French Joan was a virgin savior sent by God. To the English she was a witch sent by the Devil. While the French began to rejoice in their victory, the English pondered the magic of this female fiend. Who but someone with the power of the Devil could return to battle after being so wounded? Who but a witch could so suddenly turn the tide of war, the war in which all good Englishmen knew that God was on their side? The English were terrified of Joan. Later, when they tried to recruit more troops from England, many soldiers refused because they were afraid of Joan's sorcery, which they were sure made her invincible.

On Sunday, May 8, the morning after the great victory, watchmen on the city walls could see the English packing equipment and abandoning their fortifications. But then, as though impelled to make a last show of bravado before the French, they were seen lining up in defensive battle array. Putting on a coat of chain mail (her wound prevented her from using the heavier plate armor) Joan rode out of town with a contingent of knights and men-at-arms to confront the enemy. When an eager French knight asked Joan if they could attack, she forbade it. Soon the English turned and marched away. Joan said, "Let them go in peace. You will get them another day."

The seven-month siege of Orléans was over. It had taken only three days of fighting under Joan's inspiration to end it, and the first part of Joan's mission was accomplished. From then on, to this day, May 8 would be celebrated in Orléans with a procession of people carrying lighted candles through the town and to the scenes of battle. Though Joan's impact on the battle of Orléans was more psychological than military, it was crucial to the French victory. She had contributed what was most needed; she had raised the flagging spirits of the French and had inspired them to outdo themselves in courage and daring. Many problems still lay ahead but this was a turning point in the war.

5

❦

THE BATTLE OF PATAY

"You have good spurs. Use them."

The next part of Joan's mission was to have the Dauphin crowned King. Joan felt sure that once Charles was crowned and anointed with holy oil, all of France—even the zone occupied by the English and the Burgundian traitors—would rally to its rightful King. After that, expelling the English would be easy.

On May 9, the day after raising the siege of Orléans, Joan, Count Dunois, and an army contingent went to report to the Dauphin. They found him in his castle at Loches between Orléans and Chinon. Royalty moved from castle to castle frequently. When living within the dank stone walls became too unpleasant from the stench of pet animals, hunting dogs, and falcons, to say nothing of rarely washed human bodies, the whole court moved to another castle. Like Chinon, Loches was an ancient feudal castle, but recently it had been renovated with larger windows to replace the old narrow slits that had only dimly lighted the interior. Doorways too were enlarged, no doubt to accommodate the ever-larger women's hats.

A contemporary chronicler reported that Joan bowed low upon meeting the Dauphin, that he told her to rise and "was so overjoyed that he would have liked to kiss her." That was, perhaps, expecting too much from the diffident, hesitating Charles. In fact Charles, though impressed by the miraculous recovery of Orléans, seemed incapable of deciding what to do next. Some of his courtiers thought they should follow up their military advantage and attack the heart of the English occupied zone, Normandy; others felt they should head for Paris, where the citizens, chafing under foreign rule, would join their side. Still others felt they should first capture all the towns held by the English in the Loire River area, and then head north to Reims, where the crowning of Charles as King of France would take place. Charles's current court favorite, the obese Georges Tremoille, wanted to try for a peace treaty with the Burgundians right away. Tremoille had no use for war, even for a just cause. He preferred to use bribery or other devious means to avoid confrontation—anything so that he could stay put and enjoy the luxury of court life. He despised Joan for her lowly birth and was jealous of her sudden rise to fame.

Joan, as usual, grew impatient as precious time was wasted in what seemed to her endless, inconclusive talks. After two weeks of waiting for the Dauphin's decision, she and Lord Dunois knocked on the door of the royal chamber where Charles was in conference. Kneeling and embracing his legs as was the custom, she said, "Noble Dauphin, do not hold such lengthy council, but come to the city of Reims to receive your worthy crown."

Still Charles hesitated, during which time one of his courtiers asked Joan if she had been ordered by her "counsel" to say this. Joan was also urged to talk about her divinely sent messages. Embarrassed, she grew red in the face but answered that when things went badly and no one would believe her, she prayed to find out what to do. And she had just received a clear message that said: "Daughter of God, go, go, go. I will help you, go." Joan's advice prevailed, and it was decided to go to Reims after securing the English-held strongholds in the area, thereby clearing the way for a safe passage. Charles may have remembered that Joan had told him earlier that she would last only a little over a year; it would be foolish to lose the chance of continuing her great success.

The dashing young duke of Alençon was now given the military command, though the Dauphin ordered him to seek Joan's advice in all matters. Joan could hardly get away from the crowds of people in Loches who pressed around her, wanting a word or a touch from the heroine. When a churchman reproved Joan for allowing this "idolatry," she admitted that she didn't know how to cope with such adoration but felt that God would protect her from letting it go to her head.

Joan, Alençon, Dunois, La Hire, and other leading knights met in Orléans to plan the new campaign. Joan was now surrounded by the cream of knighthood. She was in her element with these vigorous and active young warriors who responded so enthusiastically to her own desire for action. Alençon, of royal blood, became a close friend of Joan's, the most favored of her loyal knightly followers. Young and handsome, he was to her the perfect chivalrous knight. She called him her "beau duc."

The army of some two thousand mounted knights, followed by their squires and archers, set off on June 11 for their first objective, the English-held town of Jargeau. But when they

got the dreaded report that the English Captain Fastolf was on his way with reinforcements, they feared they would be outnumbered. Nobody seemed to know just where Fastolf was, but the French were sure he was near. Joan could not understand all this panic, and forcefully reminded her companions that it didn't matter how outnumbered they were, that if they fought with spirit and determination, God would give them victory. With some misgivings, Alençon agreed to attack Jargeau.

By the second day the French had made little progress, and Alençon expressed doubts about continuing. "Ah, gentle Duke, are you afraid?" asked Joan, reminding him that she had promised his wife she would return him safe and sound. Encouraged, he returned to the assault. In the thick of battle Joan came to his side and told him to move from where he was or, she said, pointing to a cannon on the rampart, "that engine will kill you." A little later, a cannonball hurtled through the air and killed another French knight on that very spot. Then, as Joan was scaling a ladder, a small cannon stone struck her standard, rebounded onto her helmet, and knocked her to the ground. But she quickly recovered, calling out, "Up, friends, up. The English are ours." And the French swept over the walls and took the town.

As the battle drew to an end, an English commander, Lord Suffolk, was still fighting for his life against a young French squire. Unwilling to surrender to anyone ranked below knighthood, he offered to knight his young enemy and, tapping him on the shoulder, did so on the spot. His social standing saved, Suffolk then willingly surrendered. The victorious French re-

Sculpture of head in a helmet, once thought to be Joan but now thought to be St. Maurice. Photographie Bulloz, Orléans — Musée Historique, Paris.

turned again to Orléans. The mopping-up process of the Loire strongholds had begun auspiciously.

Joan's reputation soared. Far away, an Italian merchant wrote in a letter of the "wondrous things" he had heard of a young girl from Lorraine and her amazing feats at the battle of Orléans. "It is making me crazy," he wrote. He found the news all quite unbelievable, yet he felt it must be true. He concluded, "I believe God's power is great." Volunteers, men from all walks of life, poured into Orléans to join the Maid and her army—they liked to think of it as *her* army. Soon two more English strongholds were taken, forcing the enemy to withdraw their forces and retreat to the north.

Before the French pursued the retreating English, Joan met the former Constable of France, a controversial character who unexpectedly appeared with a band of tough mercenary knights, hoping to join the army. His sudden appearance threw some of the French nobles into a panic since the Constable, Count Richemont, was in disgrace and had been dismissed from Charles's court in a palace intrigue, no doubt started by his rival, Tremoille. Alençon and other nobles were under orders to have nothing to do with Richemont. They didn't trust him and didn't know if he had come to make trouble or to offer help. Joan decided to talk to him. "I did not ask you to come, but since you have come, you shall be welcome." Richemont replied, "I do not know if you are from God or not. If you are from God I fear nothing from you for God knows my good will. If you come from the Devil I fear you even less." Joan seems to have been pleased with this direct statement and soon all agreed to welcome his support.

The next day a messenger dashed up to report that Fastolf had finally joined forces with the English commander Talbot near the little village of Patay about eighteen miles to the north. The French army actually outnumbered the English now by about three to one, but the French knew only too well how often their superior forces had been beaten in open battle by the English. And the coming confrontation with the English would be open warfare, very different from the siege of a town.

The French still thought of war as an extended knightly tournament. Their custom was to wait politely while the English picked an advantageous high spot and set up a defensive barricade of pointed stakes with well-trained longbowmen stationed behind them. The English longbow could shoot arrows a distance of one hundred fifty yards with great force at a rate of ten a minute. Only when the English were ready to be attacked did the French mounted knights charge, to be met by a barrage of arrows that often killed or wounded their horses. Many of the French knights were forced to dismount and to stagger helplessly in their heavy armor in an uphill attack. The closer they came, the greater the force of the English arrows, which whizzed at them incessantly, sometimes even penetrating their armor. Any of the mounted knights who got through to the barricade were likely to be impaled on the sharp-pointed stakes.

With their pride of class and love of the old chivalric warfare, the French never thought of changing their obsolete methods. Hence their fear of confronting the English in the open. Alençon consulted Joan, who said, "You have good spurs. Use them." Did she mean them all to run away? "No," she replied. "It is the English who will not be able to defend themselves and who will be conquered, and you will need good spurs to overtake them." She predicted a great victory for the French. Sending scouts ahead to find out where the English were, La Hire

Battle of Patay. French on the left, English at right. Miniature painting from Chronique du Règne de Charles VII. Giraudon/Art Resource, Bibliothèque Nationale, Paris.

assembled the troops to be ready to move at a moment's notice. But the clumps of woods and brush that studded the area made it difficult for the scouts to spot the enemy.

Meanwhile, the English, none too confident themselves after their recent reverses, were preparing an ambush in a valley near the village of Patay where trees and dense shrubs would provide cover. They expected the French to come this way and to fall into their trap. Fastolf's men had begun to set up a line of defense on a slight rise. At the same time, Talbot's archers—stationed lower down where the pass narrowed—had just started to make the barricade of pointed stakes, when suddenly a stag leaped out of the woods and bolted past them. The archers, unaware of the nearby French scouts, couldn't resist taking a shot at such a prize—what good English yeoman could—and let loose their shafts, yelling and whooping with excitement. The noise revealed the enemy's whereabouts, and the scouts rushed back to report their discovery to La Hire, who was already on the move with the vanguard, followed by the main French army. What happened next was quick and violent. The cavalry poured into the narrow pass and cut the unprepared English enemy to pieces. Fastolf and some of his men panicked and escaped into the forest, but two thousand lay dead and two hundred were taken prisoner. Only a handful of French were killed. The much-feared Fastolf had disgraced himself to the extent that Shakespeare later depicted him as a cowardly buffoon, the fat, hard-drinking companion of Prince Hal, later Henry V, and changed his name from Fastolf to Falstaff.

The battle of Patay was over in what seemed a matter of minutes. When Joan arrived with the rear guard, she was overwhelmed at the sight of so much slaughter. It was an extraordinary reversal of the war with the English. It showed the French that speed and taking the enemy unawares could reverse the age-old English successes in open battle. Though Joan had not been involved in the fighting, she had fired the French to press forth boldly no matter what the odds. She seemed to have an instinct to know when to strike—in this case before the enemy had time to prepare. Actually the odds were with the larger French army. What had been so lacking before was spirit and good sense. Henceforth the English longbow and defensive barricades lost their effectiveness. The French had learned a lesson. Abandoning their outmoded ways, they no longer politely waited for the enemy to be ready but took to sudden, surprise attacks. The common sense of a peasant girl and the courage she inspired had a good deal to do with this.

Joan, Alençon, and others of the French army spent the

night in the village of Patay. When their prize prisoner, Talbot, was brought before them, Alençon remarked that the English must have been surprised at the outcome of the battle. The stoical Talbot simply answered, "It is the fortune of war." And so it was that the fortunes of war were beginning to change. The French were gaining confidence as the English were beginning to lose it.

6

TO CROWN THE KING

"You are the true king and . . . the kingdom of France belongs to you."

Not only Joan but all the common folk of France knew that a man was not a king until he had been consecrated and crowned in the cathedral of Reims. Joan believed strongly that the coronation was essential to Charles's success, that it would wash away the shame he had endured as a disinherited prince living in exile and would give him the prestige he needed to make France whole again.

Charles agreed with Joan about the importance of being crowned king but, as usual, was in no hurry. With his fat friend and court favorite, Tremoille, he retired to a castle on the Loire, to avoid meeting Constable Richemont. Richemont had sent him messages asking to be reinstated, saying he was eager to serve Charles. Tremoille, fearing he would lose his position to this rival, persuaded Charles to refuse to see Richemont ever again. So due to politics, the royal party lost the benefit of a great soldier and his well-trained knights. Despite this loss, the army kept swelling with volunteers eager to serve Charles and the Maid.

Back in Orléans, waiting for Charles to make a move, Joan received a token of recognition for her services to the town. The Duke of Orléans, taken prisoner by the English years before and still imprisoned in the Tower of London, sent an order for an elegant robe of fine cloth in his town's colors, crimson and green, to be tailored for Joan.

A few days later and shortly before they set off for Reims, Joan had an emotional meeting with the Dauphin. Though Charles praised her highly for all she had done, he ordered her now to rest from the terrible hardships she had endured. Did this mean he thought she had served her purpose and should now retire? Joan knew her mission wasn't finished and was so upset that she burst into tears. She told Charles he must not doubt her, that he would be crowned shortly, that he would soon have his kingdom whole again. Charles was persuaded, but the mean-spirited and jealous Tremoille couldn't stand the young peasant girl gaining favor with the Dauphin. He had gotten rid of Richemont . . . could he get rid of Joan, too?

In preparation for the march to Reims, which would have to go through Anglo-Burgundian towns, Joan sent a letter to the Duke of Burgundy urging him not to resist and inviting him to join them at the coronation. The Duke didn't answer, nor did he return her herald. It was risky business being one of Joan's heralds!

By the end of June the march to Reims finally got under way. The first town to hold up the royal party was Auxerre, where Joan had stopped to hear mass four months earlier on her way to meet the Dauphin. Then she had been trying to conceal her identity; now she was coming proudly at the head of an army in the company of royalty. But Auxerre, so long under Anglo-Burgundian rule that its citizens had become used to it, refused to open their gates to the French. Joan wanted to force them to, but instead, Tremoille managed to make a secret deal with the town's leaders and accepted a bribe of two thousand gold pieces on condition the French would not attack. Relieved, the city surrendered.

The next trouble spot en route to Reims was the large town of Troyes where Charles's mother, Queen Isabella, conniving with the Duke of Burgundy, had signed the shameless treaty disinheriting Charles and giving the French monarchy to the English. Fearful of strong resistance, Charles sent a letter to the town leaders, promising to forgive their past antiroyal behavior and to safeguard their liberties if they peacefully surrendered. Joan sent one of her straightforward "either-or" letters— either join the Dauphin or be prepared for an attack. After deliberations, the town sent out a delegation to parley with the French.

Leading the delegation was a curious emissary, Brother Richard, a wandering Franciscan friar who had been spellbinding citizens with rabble-rousing evangelistic preachings. He had drawn such crowds in Paris that the established Church, wary of his popularity, questioned his orthodoxy. He had left the city abruptly, under a cloud of suspicion for heresy. Undaunted, he was now holding sway in Troyes. He was eager to meet Joan, who he feared might be a rival or, even worse, a witch. As he came toward her, he sprinkled holy water on himself and made the sign of the cross to ward off any evil. Joan seemed to be amused and said, "Approach boldly. I shall not fly away." Brother Richard was captivated by Joan and fell on his knees before her.

Back in town Brother Richard preached a sermon urging

all to submit to the Maid and Charles. The town leaders, however, were not won over. They burned Joan's letter, and derided her as a "madwoman full of the Devil." The town gates stayed shut.

Charles and his council delayed and debated until Joan's decisive voice again prevailed. She told the council to debate no longer but to start besieging the city. "Within three days I will lead you into Troyes by love or by force or by courage, and false Burgundy will be amazed." The French began preparing the attack, filling up the city's moat with faggots and brush, as the fearful townspeople watched from their ramparts. The next day, when Joan gave the signal to attack, emissaries from the town came out to offer surrender. This bloodless victory ensured an easy march to Reims. Brother Richard tagged along, hopeful of new audiences for his preachings.

The next night was spent in Chalons, only a few miles from Reims. Here the royal party received a friendly welcome from the townspeople as well as from outsiders who were pouring in from the highways, eager to participate in the coronation march to the cathedral. Among the travelers from afar were a few from Domremy, including Joan's godfather. Joan was so glad to see him that she presented him with a red cloak she was wearing. And she confided to another old friend that she was "afraid of nothing but treason."

While Charles and Joan and the royal entourage were assembling to march to Reims, the Burgundians in charge of that city were urging the citizens to hold out against the Dauphin until their relieving army appeared. But the feelings of the people had changed—no longer would they bow to the yoke of Anglo-Burgundian rule with their true king so near and about to be crowned. The Burgundian garrison meekly departed, heading west for Paris.

On July 16, Charles arrived at Reims and lodged in the archbishop's palace. He was given the keys to the city and a pledge of the town's obedience. Preparations had to be rushed for the coronation ceremony, to be held according to tradition on Sunday, the next day. (One reason to hurry was that the town felt it could not afford to wait until the following Sunday with such a horde of soldiers and travelers to house and feed.)

All during the night before the coronation, the city resounded with the noise of carpenters hammering and of heavy wagons rumbling along the narrow cobbled streets in frantic preparation for the next day's celebration. But it was a moonlit night and the excitement was such that few cared if their sleep was disturbed.

Among the sightseers were some prominent nobles who were now convinced by Charles's recent successes that the future lay with him. They switched their allegiance from the English and Burgundians to the Royalists. Among the crowds of lesser folk were Joan's own parents, who were put up at the town's expense in an inn near the cathedral. Joan had not seen them since she left Domremy, without their permission, seven months earlier. But she had sent them messages and they had forgiven her. Now, though no doubt bewildered at seeing their daughter in the company of royalty, and dressed not in her familiar patched red peasant dress but in shining armor and a cloak of crimson and gold, they felt nothing but pride.

Early Sunday morning, July 17, 1429, the procession entered the wide portals of Reims Cathedral, one of the greatest splendors of Gothic architecture. The whole facade was encrusted with sculptures of biblical characters, angels, and saints. Though dedicated to the Virgin Mary, who was shown above the central portal being crowned, the cathedral was also the symbol of French royalty. At the highest part of the facade a row of fifty-six statues of the kings of France reinforced the sublime aura of the French monarchy. All French kings had been crowned there since the twelfth century. The cathedral was built over the spot where the first French Christian king, Clovis, had been baptized by St. Remi in the fifth century.

Charles was accompanied by Joan, who was carrying her banner. Followed by dignitaries, they walked through the central portal into the soaring nave, where the early morning sunlight shone through the stained-glass windows, casting shafts of red, blue, and gold on the columns and paved floor. It must have been breathtaking to Joan, who had never seen such a vast and ornate cathedral.

Tradition required that the twelve peers of France — six nobles and six prelates — be on hand. But owing to the war, some of these, most notably the Duke of Burgundy, were absent. Substitute dukes and bishops were hastily found to fill their places.

The ceremony took place before the high altar, where Charles prostrated himself while prayers were chanted. Then he recited the royal oath, promising to uphold the faith, defend the Church, and administer justice in ruling the kingdom entrusted to him by God. He was given the belt and spurs of chivalry, and the scepter and rod of justice. Finally came the anointment with the sacred oil believed to have been brought by a dove from heaven and so miraculous that it renewed itself after every use!

Reims Cathedral. Giraudon/Art Resource.

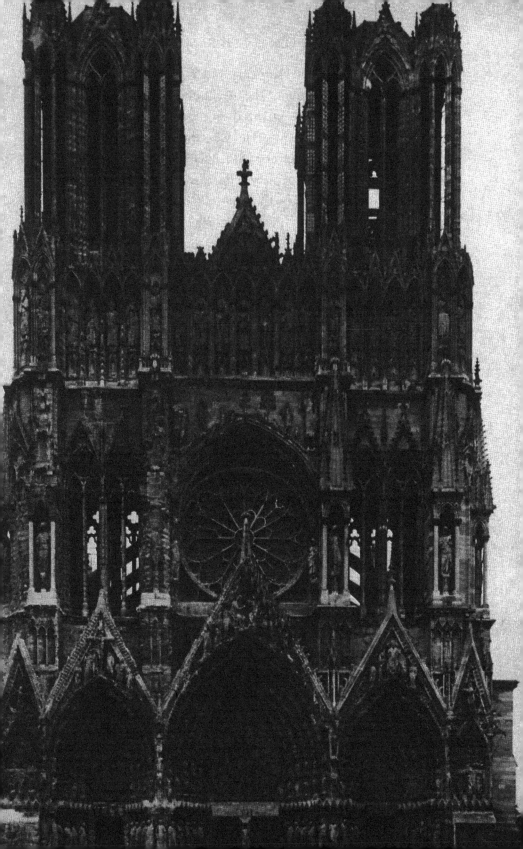

After removing the Dauphin's outer garments, leaving him in only a loose silk tunic, the Archbishop of Reims anointed Charles in five places: on his head, his chest, his back, his shoulders, and his elbows. He was then dressed again, this time in royal purple velvet studded with golden fleurs-de-lys. At last the Archbishop placed the royal crown on Charles's head. He was now King by the grace of God, the Lord's anointed. The humiliating Treaty of Troyes, which had denied him his rights, now seemed null and void to the masses of the French people.

During the long and meticulous ceremony, Joan stood beside the King holding her banner. When Joan was later asked why her banner should have been singled out for this ceremony, she answered, "It had borne the burden, it deserved the honor." Indeed all eyes were on Joan and her banner. As soon as the ceremony ended, Joan knelt before Charles and, embracing his legs, said, "Gentle King, now is done God's pleasure, Who willed that I raise the siege of Orléans and that I bring you to Reims to receive your holy consecration showing that you are true King and that the kingdom of France belongs to you." Overcome by emotion, Joan was in tears. Most of the audience was equally moved. Soon all were shouting exuberantly and the trumpets blared so loudly that some feared the vaults of the cathedral would burst asunder. Joan was at the peak of her fame.

7

⋙⋘

FALL FROM GLORY

"And thus was broken the will of the Maid. . . ."

At this moment of Joan's great glory the people of Reims went wild demonstrating their gratitude. They all knew Joan's story, her meteoric rise from a lowly peasant to a leader of nobility, and her military triumphs. And now, thanks to her, they had their own French king again. They couldn't get enough of looking at the young maid who had accomplished so much in the seven short months since she had left Domremy. They marveled at her youth and her small girlish figure encased in male armor. It all seemed incredible.

But Joan's glory was not to last. Due to circumstances beyond her control, as well as her own reactions to unfolding events, she began to lose her aura of inspired leadership.

Up to this time Joan and Charles had seen eye to eye, despite his slowness to respond to her ideas. But now there was a change in their relationship. Compared to the King, Joan was a firebrand. Her obsession to finish her task, to rout the English, clashed with Charles's slow-moving, long-range efforts

at diplomacy. His first aim was to woo the Duke of Burgundy away from his alliance with the English.

Joan also realized the value of getting Duke Philip's support. On the very day of Charles's coronation she had sent the Duke a message, earnestly begging him to desist from fighting against his true and rightful King. She expected he would now feel obliged to give allegiance to his monarch. After that she hoped he would use his power in the old royal capital, Paris, to arrange a warm welcome for the King. Once again, Joan got no answer, and decided that dealing with the Duke was a waste of time, that he could not be counted on for help. The Duke had no interest in either the English or the French except when he could use them to his own advantage.

Joan had recently expressed a fear of treachery, but she did not yet know anything about the secret deals going on behind her back. Even as her letter to the Duke was on its way, his envoys met secretly with Charles and Tremoille. The envoys offered the King a truce of fifteen days, promising to hand over Paris at the end of the truce. In reality the Duke was not about to cede Paris; he was merely playing for time. He was duly impressed by Charles's successes and new popularity, but to protect himself, he decided to play both sides. He would keep his ties with the English and at the same time make Charles think that he wanted peace. In this "double deal," he was also scheming with the English to use the fifteen days to strengthen Paris against attack.

Trusting in the truce, Charles dallied. Instead of using his military advantage and moving on Paris right away as Joan expected, he journeyed from town to town between Reims

Joan in full armor holding sword and standards. Fifteenth-century miniature painting of Joan. Archives Nationales, Paris.

and the capital. Many towns, long under Anglo-Burgundian rule, eagerly welcomed their newly crowned King. This mounting enthusiasm for Charles was all the more reason to move swiftly to the capital.

During one of these leisurely trips, when Joan was riding next to the King she asked him a favor, the only favor she ever asked of him—that he exempt her village of Domremy from royal taxes. Charles graciously granted the exemption, a privilege that would last for more than one hundred years.

Precious time was passing as Charles and his council kept making bargains with Duke Philip. During this period, so trying to Joan's patience, she and the Archbishop of Reims had a curious conversation about death and burial. He asked her where she hoped to die. Joan replied, "Wherever it pleases God, for I am sure neither of the time nor place." She added that she would be happy if God now ordered her to lay down her arms and let her return to her family in Domremy. Did this talk of home and dying mean that Joan was homesick or ready to give up the last part of her mission, that of forcing the English to leave France? Joan had certainly not changed her goal, but her mood had changed. Despite her recent glory, she sensed something was wrong. She felt a kind of letdown, as though things were slipping from her grasp.

Then Joan found out about Charles's secret truce with Burgundy. She was angry and felt betrayed. A truce was not a lasting peace and not to be trusted, especially with Duke Philip, in whom she had no faith. Without consulting Charles, she sent a message to the people of Reims. She knew they were counting on her to continue the war and to march on Paris. Expressing her fears and anxiety about the truce, she assured the citizens she would not let them down. "I am not happy with the truce and I do not know if I will keep it but if I do keep it, it will be only to preserve the King's honor. . . . I will keep the King's army together in readiness lest at the end of fifteen days they should not make peace."

Charles's council was naturally annoyed upon hearing of Joan's message to Reims. Who did this peasant girl think she was, daring to suggest she might break the King's truce? Such high-handed behavior did not help Joan's standing with Charles's courtiers nor perhaps Charles himself.

But Joan turned out to be right about the truce—Charles had been deceived. At the end of the truce there was no sign of Paris submitting. In fact, the fifteen-day truce was used to reinforce the city. Thirty-five hundred English knights and archers were now heading for Paris. With these soldiers, and after getting a huge bribe, Duke Philip felt he was best served by sticking with the English. Should Charles, however, gain ascendancy, the Duke was ready to jump to the winning side.

Letters and messages kept flying back and forth between the English, the Burgundians, and the French Royalists. Charles received an insulting one from the English regent, the Duke of Bedford, accusing him of usurping the crown of France and of using "a defamed woman, in male dress and of dissolute behavior . . . abominable to God." This truculent letter revealed not only the regent's contempt for Charles but also a deep fear of Joan, who had so suddenly changed the course of the war.

A few inconclusive skirmishes but no real battle took place between the enemies. Meanwhile Paris was being readied to withstand attack. Propaganda criticizing Charles for taking the advice of a "creature in the form of a woman called the Maid— what it was, God only knows" spread through the city. Duke

Philip himself fanned the flames of fear and hate, calling Charles a violator of the peace and warning Parisians that the French would show no mercy if they attacked the city. The easily swayed mob now swore to defend their city against any assault.

Yet Charles, who had already been duped once by his wily cousin Philip, concluded another extended truce! Short of funds to pay his army and desperately wanting peace, Charles was willing to make almost any concession to break Duke Philip's tie with England; he knew the English could not long survive in France without the help of Burgundy.

Joan, who rightly didn't trust the Duke, began to despair. She knew her time would soon run out. She wanted to make use of the spreading enthusiasm for the newly crowned King. Now was the time to march on Paris. But Charles and his court were no longer seeking Joan's advice. Though Joan remained steadfastly loyal to her King, he seemed to be distancing himself from her. Now that he was crowned, perhaps he felt he didn't need his peasant maid any longer. Joan could sense this change in their relationship. She felt rather than understood his lack of confidence and there was nothing she could do about it.

While the second truce, of which Joan knew nothing, was being arranged, Charles and his army stayed in the town of Compiègne, north of Paris. Joan, convinced that Duke Philip would respond only to a show of force, took matters into her own hands. She told Alençon that she must go to Paris. Alençon was just as eager, and they set off with a small force to the outskirts of Paris, to the suburb of St. Denis, whose abbey church was as famous as the cathedral at Reims. Kings were crowned at Reims but they were buried at St. Denis.

There is a tale that while in St. Denis, Joan, always mindful

Joan of Arc. The artist couldn't bear to depict Joan in full male armor. She looks like a sad little girl here. Fifteenth-century miniature painting. Bibliothèque Nationale, Paris.

of the knights' behavior, got angry when she saw a group of prostitutes following them. She asked the women to leave but when one wouldn't, Joan chased her and struck her with the flat of her sword, which broke in two. This was a bad omen to some, who thought she had broken her famous magical sword and thus destroyed her own miraculous power. If the tale has any truth, it may have been just an outburst of temper due to weeks of frustration. But the people would never let Joan be reduced to normal, human behavior. Everything she did had to have some aura of magic or to show some unusual portent.

It was Alençon who finally persuaded Charles to bring his army to St. Denis to help in the attack on Paris. The King was only halfhearted in his support, but there was some hope that the changeable city mob would rally to their king, especially if Joan were in the forefront. A cry went up: "She will put the King in Paris if it is left to her." The royal army moved closer to the walls of Paris and the attack began on September 8, the Festival of the Nativity of the Virgin. When Joan was later faulted for attacking on a holy day, she claimed it had not been her decision, that others were in command.

The walls of Paris were well protected, first by a deep dry ditch, then by a high earthen rampart, and finally by a wide moat full of water, too deep to wade across. Bundles of wood were hauled up to fill it for a crossing. When the assault began, Joan was on the edge of the moat, calling to the defenders on the city walls to surrender to their King Charles. She threatened they would be put to death if they did not. "Will we, you bloody tart!" shouted a crossbowman from the rampart as he shot a crossbow bolt with such force that it split Joan's armor and pierced her thigh. A minute later a second bolt hit her standard bearer in the foot. He raised his visor only to be hit again, this time between the eyes. He fell dead, dragging Joan's white standard to the ground. Joan refused to leave the battle and took shelter behind the earthen rampart. When darkness set in, she was carried away protesting that they should continue the attack, that the city would soon be theirs. She had lost none of her courage, but this time it didn't rally the knights to victory. It was said that some cursed the Maid for failing to keep her promise that they would enter Paris that night.

Joan rose early the next day, mounted her horse despite her wound, and was ready for a renewed attack. She said she would not leave until they had taken the city. Alençon and a few knights followed her. The old spirit returned for a moment. They now hoped to enter Paris at a different spot, by crossing the River Seine on a wooden bridge that Alençon had had constructed. But just as they started off, orders came from King Charles to return to St. Denis. They obeyed immediately but secretly planned to carry out the assault later. They soon found out that there would be no assault, and to their despair discovered that the King had ordered the bridge demolished in order to prevent any renewed attack. Fearing to ruin peace negotiations with Burgundy and uncertain that the populace would rally to his side, Charles and his council had decided to leave Paris alone and go back to the Loire valley to wait for peace somehow to materialize.

If Charles had wholeheartedly supported Joan and attacked Paris right after the coronation, he likely would have taken it. His long-drawn-out bargaining caused endless delays and gave the enemy time to strengthen its defenses. Yet Joan never blamed the King for letting her down. The fiasco of the Paris attack was Joan's first serious military reversal since the triumphal siege of Orléans. "And thus," wrote a chronicler, "was broken the will of the Maid and the King's army." Also broken was Joan's reputation for invincibility.

Before they left their headquarters at St. Denis, Joan removed her shining armor and laid it on the altar of the abbey church as a votive offering. Knights wounded in defense of France traditionally came to this church to donate their armor to the honor of the King and the realm. It must have been a sacrifice to part with her elegant armor. But Joan was eager to follow the knightly tradition.

Paris remained untaken, an island surrounded by the many towns that had opened their gates to Charles; at least those towns remained loyal, so some positive gains had been made. New hope for better times spread among the people.

Back in the Loire area Joan faced another bitter disappointment. Alençon, angry at Charles for giving up, departed, hoping to pursue the enemy in Normandy. He asked that Joan be allowed to go with him, but the royal council refused. And so Joan lost her "beau duc," her favorite fighting companion who had been at her side in almost every battle. She would never see him again. La Hire left too, and did what he could to harass the English in sporadic raids.

And now Joan led a strange and, for her, uncomfortable and confining life with the royal court. Used to outdoor farm work in Domremy, and then to the excitement of battles where she was surrounded by noble knights, she felt suffocated by the elegant life of royalty. She preferred the camp to the court.

From the fall of 1429 to May 1430 Joan traveled with the royal court, moving from castle to castle. She even had to stay awhile at Tremoille's château under his scornful eye. It was like being under house arrest. But if out of favor with some of the royalty, Joan was as loved and venerated by the common people as ever. In Bourges, where she stayed with a noble lady, Madame Tournolde, people kept trying to see her, to have her touch their rosaries or holy relics, hoping for a cure or some magic. It was Madame Tournolde who told how Joan had laughed at this and said that her hostess's touch would do just as much good as her own.

On one of the court peregrinations, Joan met a woman who claimed to be a visionary and who was brimming with advice. This was Catherine of La Rochelle, who told Joan that she was visited at night by a "white lady dressed in gold" who would guide them to vast treasures with which Joan could pay her men-at-arms. Joan indeed had been trying to collect money and arms hoping somehow to lead an army back to Paris. But Joan was suspicious of Catherine—in fact she told Catherine bluntly that she should go home to take care of her husband and children. However, Joan decided to test Catherine and so she spent two nights with her to see if the white lady would appear. By midnight of the first night nothing had happened, and Joan fell asleep. The next morning Catherine claimed that her lady had come while Joan slept. The second night, after carefully resting and sleeping during the day, Joan stayed awake but saw nothing. Joan decided Catherine was a fake and a liar and told the King so. Catherine probably was a fraud whose antics Joan's common sense could see through, but some thought that Joan's treatment of this visionary showed Joan couldn't tolerate a rival. And Catherine got revenge later, testifying that Joan had a pact with the Devil.

Finally the royal council stirred itself and decided to capture two towns still held by Burgundians near the Loire. Joan and another knight led the attack against the first town. She was back in her old role, her inspiration was revived, and against all odds the town was taken. Then Tremoille sent her to attack another town, held by a tough Burgundian against whom he had a personal grudge. He gave Joan scant supplies and men-at-arms, perhaps on purpose. The town's overlord was one of the few skeptics of that time—he told his garrison that they had nothing to fear from Joan, that she was not a sorceress at all, that she had no magic, either good or bad. It was, however, lack of men and supplies that forced the French to give up the siege and to retreat.

After this failure Joan was treated more as a mascot than as a God-sent leader, and many thought her inspired counsel had deserted her. Inwardly, Joan was fuming with frustration. She was getting no nearer her goal of ridding the country of the English.

By the spring of 1430, when the truce with Burgundy was about to end, Charles finally realized that he had indeed been duped by his cousin Philip. While Charles had been lulled into hopes of peace and was unprepared for war, the Duke had been using all this time to strengthen his positions up north, trying to regain towns that had gone over to Charles, even preparing to attack Reims. The drums of war were beginning to sound again. There were rumors too that a popular uprising against the enemy in Paris had been ruthlessly suppressed. It was time to stir from the idle life on the banks of the sleepy Loire.

Joan was already stirring. Hearing of the citizens of Reims's fears of a Burgundian attack, she sent a message telling them to hold out, that rescue would come soon. By April Joan herself was on her way north. How much backing she had from the King is not known. In her glorious departure for Orléans, Joan had been surrounded by many great nobles and knights. Now she had only a small band of mercenaries, her faithful squire, and her brother Pierre. It remains a mystery whether Charles sent her or just let her go. Unprepared and with his main army disbanded, maybe she was his only hope. When she left Charles, it was for the last time.

Joan went first to the Burgundian-held town of Melun, a little south of Paris. At her arrival the citizens took heart and rose in revolt. With the aid of Joan's troops, they forced the Burgundian garrison to leave.

At the very moment of this encouraging triumph, while Joan stood near the ramparts, she was overwhelmed by a feeling of foreboding, of disaster soon to come. Moments later she heard her voices, warning her that she would be captured soon, before the Feast of St. John, which took place on June 24, barely two months away. Though not unexpected—Joan had known for a long time that she had only a little more than a year to carry out her mission—this was a cruel and bitter blow. "Let me die quickly, without a long captivity," she begged, but her voices gave her no reassurance of that, nor could she learn the hour or the day she would be taken. She was urged not to be cast down, that God would help her.

How could she finish her mission in so short a time? She must act quickly and secure all towns near Paris before trying another attempt on the capital. At the town of Lagny, just east of Paris, Burgundian mercenaries were harrassing the citizens for their loyalty to Charles. Joan and her knights routed the Burgundians, and captured their leader, a noble who was also a notorious criminal. Joan hoped to exchange him for a French prisoner who had led a revolt in Paris, but found out that the Frenchman had been put to death. When the town council urged that she turn over the Burgundian leader to be tried for his many crimes, Joan agreed, saying, "Since my man whom I wanted is dead, do with this man as you ought by justice." After a two-week trial this man was condemned to death for his past crimes of murder and treason. Much was made of this episode. Some have seen it as evidence of a decline in Joan's character, or revealing a bloodthirsty cruelty. The Burgundians saw it as a breach of the code of chivalry since the condemned man was of the nobility and could have been ransomed. Joan, who had always admired chivalry, was no longer surrounded by noble knights like Alençon but by practical professional soldiers. Could they have changed her attitude? Actually the Burgundian leader was a hardened criminal. Joan had little say in the matter. But earlier on in her glorious year she might well have dared to object. The atmosphere was changed now. This and another very different episode in Lagny were held against Joan at her trial.

While in the town Joan was asked to take part in a rather astonishing medieval ritual to revive a baby thought to be dead. This practice took place in a church that had a miraculous statue of the Virgin Mary. Joan knelt before the statue along with other maidens already praying there. It was hoped that the added magic of Joan's virginity would bring the baby to life long enough for it to be baptized. Soon "the baby appeared to yawn three times." It lived just long enough to be baptized, and was quickly buried, its grateful parents assured that its soul was saved. Though this had been a joint enterprise, Joan's admirers thought it her miracle; her enemies thought it her witchcraft. Asked at her trial if the town had not credited the baby's revival solely to her "magical power," Joan replied she didn't know, she had never inquired. Whatever the truth of the story, it shows that no matter how much Joan denied being a miracle worker, her followers would have her so while her enemies would have her a user of the black arts of magic.

In early May, not long after the extended truce had formally expired, Charles openly admitted Duke Philip's duplicity, saying that the Duke "had never, and has not now any intention of coming to terms of peace, but has always favored and does favor our enemies"—all of which Joan had warned him about the summer before. Finally some of the royal army moved north. Joan joined them in some unsuccessful attacks on Burgundian-held towns. After a council of war, the army again disbanded due to shortage of money and supplies. Disappointed, Joan rode off with her small mercenary band to a town south of Compiègne. Sadly Joan later admitted that since it had been revealed to her that she would soon be captured, she had left military matters mostly to other captains of war.

Duke Philip had been gathering forces to lay siege to Compiègne, a town that had stayed steadfastly loyal to Charles. He planned to surround the town and had already captured several villages on the north bank of the little River Oise opposite Compiègne on the south shore. The commander of Compiègne, a hot-tempered man named Guillaume de Flavy, was determined to defend his town at any cost. He anxiously watched the enemy forces increasing daily across the river. Soon he could see that they had taken the village of Margny, directly opposite Compiègne, less than a mile from the little bridge between them.

On May 22 Joan learned that Duke Philip himself was closing in on Compiègne; she decided to rush to its rescue. Some of her men thought it too risky but Joan felt she must try to help the good citizens of the town. Though fifteen miles away and separated from the town by a thick forest, she started off at midnight with her small escort. The only light was the faint glimmer of a crescent moon.

Joan arrived in Compiègne at dawn, May 23. Late in the day she and about four hundred knights left the town to make a surprise attack on Margny and to secure the bridge. Commander Flavy placed gunners and crossbowmen on his town's walls and ordered boats to be readied to cover any retreat. As Burgundy's men in Margny saw the French galloping uphill toward them, they quickly sent an alarm to summon reinforcements. In the midst of fierce hand-to-hand fighting, Burgundian

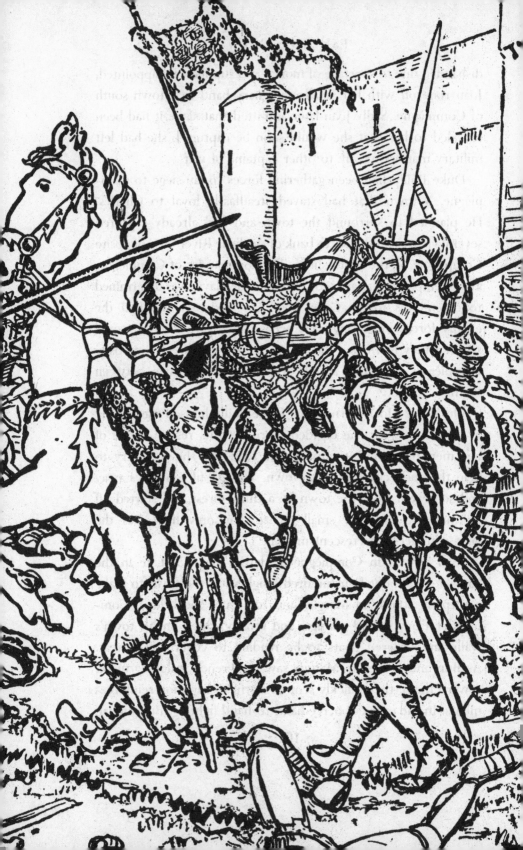

forces began pouring in from all directions. Some of the French started to panic. A cry went up, "Every man for himself! Back to the town!" Joan tried to stem the flight, but her words went unheeded as the frightened French stampeded toward the river, jumped into the boats, and scrambled back to Compiègne. Most were safely back within the city walls when Captain Flavy, fearful that the enemy might assault his town any minute, raised the drawbridge and closed the city gates. The enemy was now locked outside—but so was Joan, who, with only a handful of knights, was still fighting gallantly. Forced into a boggy field by the river, the little group was overwhelmed by superior forces, all pressing to run down the Maid. A Burgundian archer grabbed her cloak and ignominiously pulled her off her horse, shouting to her to yield. St. John's Day was still a month away but "a little more than a year" had already passed.

Though some of the French nobility had lost confidence in Joan's inspired leadership, the English and Burgundians were still so impressed with her powers that they "were more joyous than if they had seized five hundred men-at-arms, for they feared no captain or leader as much as they had . . . feared the Maid."

Capture of Joan at Compiègne. Sketch in W. P. Barrett's book *The Trial of Jeanne d'Arc.* Gotham House, Inc., 1912.

8

POOR CAPTIVE

"It is not yet time."

Joan was no ordinary prisoner. The archer who had captured her knew he had to give her up to his overlord, who in turn gave her to his overlord, Jean de Luxembourg, a passionately loyal vassal to the Duke of Burgundy. The Duke could have claimed her as his prize but instead allowed Luxembourg to hold her prisoner. Joan was immediately incarcerated in his castle of Beaulieu. And so Joan's active life of leading knights to battle came to an abrupt end.

Beyond the confines of Beaulieu another battle had begun, the battle among factions of Joan's enemies, each claiming the right to possess her. The English, who thought of her not only as a witch but as a prisoner of war, couldn't wait to get their hands on her. And there was the strong arm of the Church, the pro-Anglo-Burgundian University of Paris, seat of the most learned Church scholars of the day and considered the authority on all Church matters. Its august theologians could hardly wait to have Joan in their clutches and to try her for heresy and sorcery. One of the University's former members, Bishop Cauchon, felt she was his prize since she had been captured in his bishopric. He immediately began negotiations on behalf of the English to buy her, hoping he would be put in charge of the trial. The haggling over the fate of the prisoner went on for months.

The eagerness with which Joan's enemies tried to get hold of her contrasted sharply with the apathy of the French Royalists who did little, if anything, to help her. The person who should have tried, at whatever the cost, to rescue or ransom Joan was her own King Charles, who owed everything to her. There was a rumor that he sent an embassy to the Duke of Burgundy warning him not to hand Joan over to the English and threatening to wreak vengeance on English prisoners of war if he did. Perhaps the embassy was intercepted, perhaps it was never sent. In any case Charles did nothing open or concrete to free Joan. The Church, which was in such a hurry to try her lest she escape or be ransomed, need not have worried. The indecisive Charles lay low, ruled by his courtiers, who probably persuaded him that Joan had lost her usefulness, and that he might as well forget her. No one knows Charles's inner thoughts but without his leading knights, his army all but disbanded, and with the military courage Joan had inspired gone, Charles likely felt that his hands were tied; he would stand no chance of rescuing her from the combined might of the Anglo-Burgundian forces. Still lurking in the King's mind was his hope for peace and a fear of doing anything to anger the Duke of Burgundy. Whatever his reasons, he abandoned Joan to her fate.

The Archbishop of Reims, more a worldly politician than a true churchman, had turned against Joan after the King's coronation. Joan had become a nuisance to him, obstructing his efforts to arrange the truce with Burgundy when she insisted on attacking Paris. He found her difficult to control, a troublemaker. Although he had supported her before the Battle of Orléans and had stood at her side when he had crowned the King, he now openly declared that Joan had brought about her own downfall through pride and willfulness, and by promoting her own ideas without consulting him or the Church.

As for Tremoille, he was openly pleased at the news of Joan's capture. All along he had scorned the Maid as nothing but a peasant farmhand and had always resented her power over the King.

In contrast to the aristocratic circles and the hostility and indifference they expressed, the common people were grief stricken at the news of Joan's capture. Masses were said for her in Orléans and other towns. Processions of people walked barefoot through the streets, protesting her imprisonment.

In the castle of Beaulieu, Joan was not treated unkindly at first—she even had her page, Jean d'Aulon, nearby to tend her—but to be a prisoner at all weighed heavily on her. She was only eighteen, full of energy and longing to finish her mission. Confined in a castle tower she worried about the good people in Compiègne whom she had hoped to rescue. Worst of all was the thought that she might be sold to the English, the fate she most dreaded. She heard rumors of this scheme and it drove her to attempt an escape. Prying loose some floorboards, she squeezed through and let herself down to the ground floor. Then she made a bold attempt to lock her guards in the tower but a porter heard the key turning and sounded the alarm. After this Joan was moved to a place of greater security, Jean de Luxembourg's more imposing castle of Beaurevoir. Surrounded by moats and strong curtain walls, there would be no chance of escape or rescue there. Joan was imprisoned in one of the thick-walled towers.

Jean de Luxembourg and his family—his wife, his aunt, and his daughter—all lived in the central tower keep at Beaurevoir and frequently visited Joan. Again she was treated well and the three ladies not only were kind to her but tried to persuade Luxembourg not to sell her to the English. Joan became fond of these ladies. When they urged her to discard her male clothing and put on women's attire, she found it difficult to refuse them. But Joan did refuse, saying, "It is not yet time." She felt she would be betraying her role and letting down her voices. Also, she had not yet abandoned the possibility of rescue or escape, for which she would need men's clothes. Joan later admitted that she would sooner have taken up women's clothes at the request of these kind ladies than of anyone else.

Another visitor, not to her liking, was a Burgundian knight who visited her out of curiosity. When he tried to embrace her and feel her breasts, she angrily pushed him away. He seemed surprised that a peasant girl would react this way to a knight, but he was impressed by her modesty and purity.

In spite of the kind treatment of the Luxembourg ladies, Joan couldn't get her mind off the fate of Compiègne, the town she had so desperately tried to save. She heard that the enemy planned to kill off all its inhabitants over the age of seven.

Then word of Joan's worst fear was leaked to her: Plans had been completed to sell her to the English. Her kind lady friends had been unable to help her.

Though Joan was well guarded at Beaurevoir, she had the freedom of walking on the tower roof, sixty to seventy feet above ground, far too high to attempt an escape. But Joan was desperate now. She began to think of trying a leap from the tower even though her voices tried to restrain her. Joan argued with them, even beseeched them, but they were adamant. Finally Joan took matters into her own hands, defying her voices, and, commending herself to God, she threw herself off the tower.

Joan's guards found her lying in a dry moat, stunned and looking as though she were dead. She was unconscious but not dead; nor, miraculously, had she broken any bones. She was unable to eat or drink anything for several days, but after asking God's forgiveness and being comforted by her voices she recovered. Joan never completely denied that she had attempted suicide, which was considered a grave sin, but she claimed she did it mostly to avoid being handed over to the English and to see if she could somehow help rescue her friends in Compiègne. She probably didn't know herself whether her leap, done in a moment of anguish, was aimed at suicide or escape. It likely involved a little of both.

Later, when questioned about this desperate leap, Joan admitted she had done wrong in disobeying her voices and blamed only herself. Joan always exonerated her voices, which she felt could do no wrong; she blamed only herself whenever she did anything contrary to their advice.

So the prisoner was moved again, this time farther from the war zone. She was taken from one castle to another, always getting closer to the seat of English occupation in Normandy. She spent some time in the castle of Crotoy, at the mouth of the Somme River, high above the English Channel, where she had her first glimpse of the sea. Her hero, Alençon, had once been held prisoner there by the English but he had been ransomed

Rouen Castle. The big tower held the dungeon and instruments of torture. Joan was imprisoned in second tower to right. The Bettman Archive.

by the French Royalists. By now Joan was beginning to wonder whether she should count on any such happy outcome.

Joan had been in captivity about five months when negotiations were finally completed for her sale to the English. The University of Paris had long supported and been well rewarded by the Anglo-Burgundian establishment, thinking it more stable and prosperous than Charles's Royalist party. The theologians wanted to try Joan in Paris. This powerful group—so powerful that even popes deferred to it—was racked by deep-seated fears of heresy. It had grown suspicious of visionaries, especially those who claimed they were sent by God but who had not consulted it or Church authorities. The University and the Church would accept only those visionaries who had confided in and been approved by the Church itself. At about the time of Joan's leap from the castle tower, another female visionary had been condemned by the Church and burned at the stake—the accepted punishment for heresy or sorcery. The young woman had insisted she had direct communication with God but had failed to consult the Church. She also spoke out in favor of Joan's God-sent mission, hurting not only herself but Joan. It was just such women who the Church feared would undermine its authority and its control of people's spiritual lives. What need would there be for the clergy if visionaries like Joan could convince people that God could intervene directly through them? Added to Joan's threat to the Church were her inexplicable victories over the English, who the University of Paris felt had God on their side. Joan must be false, a liar and deceiver of the people. She could have defeated the English only by enchantment and sorcery. She must be a witch. The Church could not afford to be soft on anyone as independent and unorthodox as Joan—she was a dangerous subversive spreading heresy throughout the land.

Bishop Cauchon became England's chief negotiator in its attempt to buy Joan. Cauchon was even more political and self-serving than the Archbishop of Reims. He had enjoyed a quick rise to fame and fortune as a result of his support of the English and had been well paid for his help in drafting the Treaty of Troyes, which had given them the French crown. And he had a personal grudge against Joan and King Charles, whom he blamed for forcing him out of Beauvais and taking over his bishopric. Like the English, he feared Joan's fiendish power but was sure he could find enough evidence of her sorcery or heresy to have her condemned to death. He knew his Church law well, and if he could prove Joan a heretic or witch, he would also prove that Charles had been led astray by sorcery, that his crowning was invalid. The English were pleased to have this adroit and impeccable bishop in charge. They hoped to kill two birds with one stone—get rid of Joan and discredit Charles. The trial would make Joan's death legal and at the same time make Charles's claim to the French throne illegal. Through guilt by association, Charles himself would suffer the taint of heresy and witchcraft. Heresy and witchcraft had come to be almost synonymous since both implied abandoning God.

The English felt they could count on Cauchon to do the job and they would pay him well. They even agreed to pay for the trial itself.

Even so, the money to buy Joan was slow in coming. Taxes had to be raised and collected and Jean de Luxembourg was holding out for a good price for his rare prisoner. However, by the time Joan was in the castle of Crotoy, Luxembourg had been paid ten thousand gold crowns, and it had been decided to try her in Rouen, Normandy, the seat of English power. Paris was felt to be too dangerous, too close to Royalist sympathizers.

In December, a few days before Christmas and seven months after her capture, Joan was taken by boat across the mouth of the Somme River, thence in stages to the city of Rouen. Her days of kindly treatment were over.

9

SETTING THE STAGE
FOR THE TRIAL

"A beautiful trial."

Heavily guarded and tied by ropes to a horse, Joan was led through the gates of Rouen, a city whose hills slope gently down to the Seine River, forming a sort of amphitheater. Rivaling Paris in beauty and wealth, Rouen had been occupied by the English for about twelve years. It had become so English that it seemed a second London. When Joan entered the town, it swarmed with English soldiers under the command of the English Earl of Warwick. Such was the fear of Joan that the Earl had been alerted to see that there would be no popular demonstration in her support and no chance of her escaping. Crowds lined the streets to get a glimpse of the famous girl-warrior who had so damaged the English cause. If any of the subjugated French wished to cheer her, they dared not.

Joan was taken to the ancient royal castle built in the thirteenth century to withstand an earlier invasion of English armies. High above the bustling town, the castle was built around an inner court with seven huge towers projecting from its massive walls. Only one tower, with the dungeon and its instruments of torture, remains today. Built against the inner walls of the oval courtyard were the great hall for royal gatherings, kitchens, servants' quarters, the royal chapel, and royal suites for young King Henry VI (though only eight years old he had already been crowned King of England) and his regent, the Duke of Bedford. The Earl of Warwick, who had all sorts of jobs—tutor to the boy king, captain of the castle guards, and Joan's special watch-dog—shared the royal suites. Though so close to each other, little King Henry, secure in the royal nursery, and Joan, secured by chains in her tower, would never meet.

When Joan heard she was going to be tried by the Church, she begged to be put in a church prison where she would be tended by nuns. Instead, she was shut up in one of the castle towers whose walls were twelve feet thick; only a thin ray of light penetrated its dark interior through a narrow slit high up in the thick wall. As if this were not enough to prevent her from escaping, Joan was chained to a heavy log and had five coarse Englishmen guarding her day and night. They not only tormented her, telling her at one time that she would be saved, and at another that she would suffer death, but also molested her and even tried to rape her. She clung to her male clothing desperately, lacing her long hose as tightly as she could, hoping that it would offer some protection.

There were many irregularities about Joan's trial and im-prisonment. Though she was to be tried by the Church, she was denied her right of being in a church prison, where she would have better treatment. Though the English considered her a prisoner of war of the greatest political importance, they treated her as a common criminal. And though the Church was going to try her, the English were going to pay for the trial.

There was another irregularity. Bishop Cauchon was Bishop of Beauvais and had the right to try cases only in his bishopric. The English sidestepped this rule and granted him the right to try Joan in Rouen. Cauchon hoped to be appointed Archbishop of Rouen as a reward for his work.

Cauchon knew that all Christendom awaited his verdict. He laid careful plans for the trial, which he said would be a "beau procès," a beautiful trial. Perhaps some might think it beautiful, but few would call it just. In his thorough way he sent scouts to gather evidence against Joan. For a trial of heresy, any kind of slanderous gossip or hearsay against the suspect was allowed as evidence, and no proof was required. But the scouts that Cauchon sent to Domremy and its neighboring villages found nothing they could use against her. When one man reported that he found "nothing in Joan which he would not wish to find in his own sister," Cauchon accused the man of being a traitor. Whatever information was gathered proved disappointing as evidence against Joan and was not put in the trial record. But Cauchon felt that Joan's reputation among the English and Burgundians for her evil doings was sufficient evidence. And he was sure he could make good use of what he had learned of Joan's childhood activities and her village customs. Village beliefs in those backward rural areas were always suspect, what with their fairies' trees and healing waters, their "wise women" who cured people with herbs and enchantments. It was in the folk religion of the countryside that subversive heresies so often arose and terrified the established Church.

To give the trial the prestige befitting its serious charges of heresy, Cauchon called on the Inquisition, the special tribunal for trying such cases. He hoped to enlist the Grand Inquisitor of the Faith and of Heretical Error himself, but unfortunately for Cauchon the Grand Inquisitor was otherwise occupied in Rome. The bishop had to settle for the Sub-Inquisitor, Jean Le Maître, who proved to be another disappointment. Le Maître was reluctant to serve at the trial, and only under threats from the English did he agree. Even so he showed up only occasionally.

Among the churchmen Cauchon solicited were a few who dared to criticize the trial. One pointed out that Joan had already been examined and proven innocent by the Church two years earlier, before being allowed to march on Orléans. Another one who objected to the irregularities of the trial proceedings was arrested at Cauchon's orders; and a third cleric left town after suggesting that the trial was unfair and one-sided, that it proceeded more from hatred than from a desire for justice. He knew the English planned to do away with Joan no matter what was proved and that they were happy to let Cauchon run the trial as long as they could count on her being condemned to death.

Despite these annoying setbacks for Cauchon, he managed to gather a large group of learned churchmen, some of whom feared to refuse to serve, some from the University of Paris who were only too eager, and others who hoped to gain English favor and pay. There were sixty in all, including clerks to take down the minutes. Most of the members were to act as consultants or advisors. Cauchon and Le Maître were to be the sole judges. A friend of Cauchon's, Jean d'Estivet, was named promoter or prosecutor. Harsh and cruel, he insulted Joan whenever he could, calling her a harlot and a blasphemer.

Joan had no defense lawyer or advisor of any sort. She who could neither read nor write would have no help at all in answering the barrage of intricate questions from the learned

doctors of law and theology. She had no witnesses to call upon. In the modern American system of justice, the accused is considered innocent until proved guilty; Joan, in contrast, like all defendants in heresy trials, was presumed guilty unless she could prove her innocence. There would be no appeal from the final verdict.

While Cauchon was finishing his long-drawn-out preparations for the trial, Joan was examined once more for her virginity. She invited this herself upon being asked why she called herself the "Maid." She answered, "I can well say that I am so, and if you don't believe me, have me examined by women." She was examined under the direction of the English Duchess of Bedford and again pronounced a true virgin. But the judges never mentioned this proof in the trial record, and it didn't stop them from insinuating she was a whore and a witch though everyone knew a virgin could be neither. And though the Duchess had given strict orders that Joan's guards were to make no sexual advances, they continued to harass her. Once she screamed and the Earl of Warwick came to her rescue.

While she waited for the trial to begin she had many visitors, some just curious to see the famous "witch-girl." With so many guards and all these visitors coming and going, Joan was hardly alone, but she was completely friendless, surrounded only by enemies. She found it difficult to hear her voices, usually so consoling to her, with the continuous loud-mouthed taunting of her guards.

The Inquisition, which had been called in on this case, had originally been set up to combat heresy, to bring sinners back to the true Catholic faith, and to save people's souls from hell. The aim of an Inquisition trial was to uncover thoughts

Medieval court of justice. Miniature painting. Giraudon/Art Resource.

and opinions, point out any errors of faith, and extract an admission of guilt from the accused. A confession of crime was considered proof of guilt no matter how it was obtained. Almost anything was fair game in persuading a person to confess—spies, torture, and deceit were used freely. With psychological cunning, inquisitors probed the very soul of the accused, and by subtle, devious questions that they asked over and over again in different ways they hoped to trap their victim into confession. Like the tentacles of a giant octopus, they gradually closed in on their prey, squeezing out an admission of guilt.

Next to Joan's prison cell was a tiny anteroom with a spy hole through which whatever she said could be heard. One of Cauchon's most despicable assistants, Loiseleur, pretending to be sympathetic—even disguising himself as a friendly peasant from Joan's countryside—tried to extract damaging information from her while two other assistants listened in the anteroom.

By the middle of January 1431, shortly after Joan had turned nineteen, Cauchon began a series of meetings with his assistants, reading out the accusations he had drawn up. He read aloud letters of the University of Paris, of the English, of the Inquisition, and some of his own to show the widespread concern for Joan's false doctrines and other evils she had been spreading through the land. He expressed his gratitude to the Church for having chosen him to defend and uphold the holy Church and the Catholic faith against Joan's transgressions. The stage was now set for the trial. Backed by the power of England, Cauchon was sure of the outcome. The one thing Cauchon and his group had not considered was the caliber of their prisoner.

10

❦

ON TRIAL

"You may ask me such things as I will not tell you."

By February 21 Cauchon was ready with his evidence against Joan. He had a long list of her so-called crimes: wanton behavior, unseemly male dress, heretical beliefs, and, from English and Burgundian sources, tales of her sorcery and witchcraft. To satisfy the English, Cauchon had to prove that Charles was not the rightful King of France, and that he had been led astray by a false, deceitful sorceress who claimed to be sent by God when, in fact, she was a tool of the Devil.

At eight o'clock on that February morning Joan, dressed in a black tunic and long tightly laced hose, was led by the usher, Massieu, from her cell, through the courtyard, and up the steps to the royal chapel for the first public hearing. Joan had no idea what she would be questioned about nor did she know how long the trial would last. By medieval standards it was unusually long and exhaustive; Joan's trial went on for three months, from late February to late May. Morning sessions of about three hours were often continued in the afternoon. It was an ordeal that would have taxed even the toughest and most clever person.

Joan had asked to hear mass before the opening of the trial, but her request had been denied because of her alleged crimes and her wearing of men's clothes. However, Massieu showed more sympathy than others and often let Joan pause to say a prayer at the chapel door en route to wherever the court met—it changed places often.

Facing the large assemblage of learned churchmen, most of whom she had never seen, Joan appeared confident and calm. It did not take long for the tribunal to find out that the young prisoner was no cowering little simpleton. Joan was asked to swear on the Gospels that she would tell the truth in answer to everything she would be asked. Joan spoke out boldly. "I do not know what you may question me about. Perhaps you may ask me such things as I will not tell you." Requested again in slightly different words to answer truthfully all questions concerning the faith and everything else she knew, Joan replied that she would gladly swear to tell the truth about her family and all she had done since leaving home but that she would not tell anything about her revelations from God. She said she had told these things to no one except King Charles, and that even if they threatened to cut off her head she would not talk about her visions. The churchmen were a little taken aback but perhaps somewhat mollified when Joan added that she would let them know in a week if she would be allowed to disclose more. Finally Joan agreed to swear on the Gospels to tell the truth about everything asked her concerning the faith but nothing about her revelations. The court settled for her limited oath.

Then the questions came thick and fast touching on a wide

Louis Maurice Boutet de Monuel, *The Joan of Arc Series: The Trial of Joan of Arc,*
1911, 29 ¾ x 67 ½, oil and gold leaf. In the Collection of The Corcoran Gallery
of Art, Washington, D.C. William A. Clark Collection.

range of subjects, many designed to confuse Joan or to make
her contradict herself. Sometimes several churchmen questioned
her at the same time or interrupted her answers. Cauchon's
"beautiful trial" was not exactly orderly that first day. At one
point Joan objected. "Fine lords, ask one at a time." The clerk,
Manchon, who was taking down the minutes, grew angry at
the tumult. And he objected when he noticed other clerks
changing Joan's answers, omitting some of her explanations.
He also objected that there were two men hidden behind a
curtain, writing their own version of Joan's replies, and finally
put a stop to it.

In answer to questions about her faith, Joan emphasized
that she had learned all her religion from her mother, who
had taught her the Lord's Prayer, the Hail Mary, and the
Catholic creed. Cauchon then told Joan to recite the Lord's
Prayer. "I will not say it unless you hear me in confession,"
replied Joan. Cauchon may have been trying to trap Joan, for
it was thought that no witch could get through the Lord's
Prayer without stumbling and surely this uneducated girl would

stumble. But Joan's demand for a confession put him on the spot. She thought she could convince him that she was a good Catholic and that he would then absolve her. And he may have feared just that. Or he may have felt that the Joan whom he considered a heretic should not have the benefit of any religious service. He dodged the issue by offering two other churchmen to hear her recite the prayer. But Joan refused unless first heard in confession. Soon the matter was dropped.

Just before the end of this first session, Joan complained about being kept in irons. Cauchon explained that it was necessary to keep her from escaping, as she had tried in other prisons. Joan admitted she had wanted to escape and still did, and asserted that it was the right of any prisoner of war—she thought of herself as a captive of the English. She said she had never given an oath *not* to try to escape so that if she *did* escape she could not be faulted for breaking her word. On account of this, orders were given to her guards to allow no one to speak to her without permission and to watch her more strictly than ever. There was a real fear that Joan might escape through sorcery.

The next day's session and the four following were held in a small room next to the great castle hall. At each of these sessions Joan was told again to swear to answer truthfully to everything asked, but she continually refused to answer questions about her revelations. She protested that she had sworn enough, that her judges should be satisfied. She added, "You overburden me too much." When they persisted, she said, "You may ask me such things that as to some, I shall tell the truth, as to others not." As though issuing a threat she said, "If you were well informed about me, you would wish that I were out of your hands. I have done nothing except by revelation." She adamantly stuck to this point of view in spite of being warned she was endangering herself. She said that if she gave the oath they wanted, she might say something she had sworn not to reveal and would thus perjure herself. So, day after day, she gave only her limited oath.

When asked something she did not want to answer, she would often say, "Pass on," or "I will not answer that; it has nothing to do with the trial." Sometimes when she felt she didn't know how to answer, she would postpone a reply, saying "I will let you know in a week if I have permission to tell you." Right from the start Joan had set a tone of defiance that her judges interpreted as a cover-up of some evil; whereas Joan was simply trying to be true to herself and above all to protect her sacred voices. Her direct and sincere answers only antagonized the churchmen. Someone pointed out that if Joan had said "It seems to me" instead of "I know for certain," she might have fared better.

The doctors of law and religion soon began to press her on her voices and her wearing of men's clothes, two areas they came back to again and again. It wasn't that the churchmen didn't believe in visions or supernatural voices—their goal was to prove that Joan's voices came from the Devil, not from God, as Joan insisted. Since Joan had kept her voices so secret and had not had them approved by the Church, not even by her village priest, they were suspect. How could they be from God when Joan had disobeyed her parents, run away from home, and dressed like a man—all sins according to the Church and the Bible. Either Joan was lying or had been deceived by the Devil. Asked who had ordered her to dress like a man, Joan said she blamed no one but herself. Asked the same question later in an attempt to make her contradict herself, Joan said, "dress is but a small matter and that she had not been advised to take it by any living man." She implied that God would not care about such a little thing as dress, and added that she had not had any message that God disapproved of her male clothes. She asked that they look at the record in Poitiers, where churchmen had approved her and her male dress. Joan was a bit naive to think that these English-paid doctors would deign to look at the records of their enemy.

Nearly all the questions somehow led back to Joan's voices, the subject that Joan so wanted to avoid. Though at first she refused to discuss them, the subtle questioning gradually wormed out information about her private spiritual life. Before the trial, Joan had never described her voices in detail, except perhaps to Charles. How could she make explicit her indescribable supernatural experiences to these learned men? It was not easy for an unlettered peasant girl to put into words heavenly visions that appeared to her in a flash of light. She was being asked to define the indefinable. It seemed beyond her, and Joan resisted as long as she could. She had usually referred to her divine messages as her "counsel," or just simply announced that she was acting at God's command.

But step by step her inquisitors wore her down. Asked if she had heard her voices recently, Joan said she had the day before, that she had been awakened by one of them. Did the voice wake her by touching her? (Could a voice *touch*? The judges were trying to make her admit some physical, nonspiritual contact.) Joan denied any touch but said that the voice told her to answer her inquisitors boldly and that God would help her. After several more irritating questions, Joan looked directly at Bishop Cauchon and said, "You say you are my judge. Consider well what you do, for in truth I am sent by God and you put yourself in great peril." This bold, threatening remark was hardly what the Bishop expected from a peasant girl on trial for her life.

Asked if her voices could see, Joan answered, "I am not going to tell you everything." She said she was more afraid of displeasing her voices than of her judges. A few minutes later came the same question asked differently: "Do the voices have eyes?" Joan answered, "You will not know that yet," and added a curious remark: "There is a saying among little children that people are often hanged for telling the truth." This saying might have been heard in Joan's war-torn village as a warning to children not to tell anything to strangers lest they turn out to be enemies. By now Joan was becoming more and more convinced that her pro-English judges were enemies, while they grew more and more convinced that she was not telling the truth.

In a sudden switch to a different subject, a difficult theological question designed to trap her, Joan was asked if she was in a state of grace, meaning free of all sin. This was tricky for Joan. If she said yes, she would be presumptuous—only God could know if a person was in a state of grace. If she said no, she would admit to being in a state of sin. One inquisitor objected to this question as unanswerable, but Joan had an answer, her most famous: "If I am not, may God put me there; if I am, may God keep me there. I would be the most miserable person in the world if I knew I were not in God's grace." And she doubted that she could hear her voices if she were in a state of sin. The court was quite stupefied by Joan's wise response.

Then back to the voices. The tortuous questions finally forced Joan to be more expansive than she wanted. Her private spiritual life had now been invaded and she felt she had to make her voices more concrete, to name them. It seemed the only way to make her inquisitors believe that her voices truly came to her from God through His saints.

It was after being asked if her voices were voices of angels, whether they were male or female, and whether they came straight from God, that Joan finally named them. Two, she said, belonged to St. Margaret and St. Catherine, saints she had confided in since early childhood. Remembering their statues or how she saw them in mystery plays, she said they were richly and beautifully crowned. St. Michael, the royal patron saint and archangel, was the third voice. This led to questions about how her saints were dressed and just what they looked like. Though Joan now said, "I saw them with my own eyes as well as I see you," she refused at first to give any more details, insisting only that they were real and were sent to her by God. Always preceded by a bright light, they gave her much comfort and filled her with great joy.

Still more specifics were wanted and she was asked what parts of her saints she saw. And now poor Joan was on a slippery path leading her onto dangerous ground. The more she described her saints in order to identify them, the more she convinced her judges that her saints were demons in disguise, just what they wanted to prove. For the Church held that saints were ethereal and did not show themselves physically; only demons disguised as saints could do that.

In answer to what part of her saints she saw, she said their faces, she didn't know if she saw their arms and legs. Did they have hair? Joan snapped back in their defense, "It is good to know they did." The doctors were out to prove she had some impure sensuous relationship with her saints. They asked her if St. Michael appeared to her naked. Joan answered, "Do you think God cannot afford to clothe him?" And to "Did Michael have hair?" she replied, "Why should it be cut off?" These witty answers didn't stop the learned men and they went right on. Did her saints smell nice? Joan assured them that they did. Did she kiss or embrace them? When Joan said she embraced them, she was asked if she felt any warmth from their bodies, and replied, "I could not embrace them without feeling and touching them." And then, "What part of their bodies did she embrace?" "It is more fitting to embrace their feet than their bodies," said Joan, who had learned that embracing a lord around his ankles was the customary act of deference.

Asked if St. Margaret spoke English, Joan said, "Why should she speak English when she is not on the English side?" This patriotic French remark did not amuse the pro-English court. When asked if her saints hated the English, she had a quick answer: "They love what the Lord loves, and hate what He hates." Joan could still hold her own. When asked if God hated the English, Joan said she did not know; she knew only that the English would be driven out of France.

A few of the doctors were impressed by Joan's pithy answers and by her good memory. Sometimes she recalled being asked questions that her judges had already forgotten. Once she protested that she had answered a certain question eight days earlier. When a clerk denied it, the record was checked and Joan was proved to be right. The clerk admitted his mistake, at which Joan playfully remarked that she would pull his ears if he did it again. Such light moments were unusual, and Joan's peasant humor was rarely appreciated.

Questioning Joan about her youth in Domremy, her in-

The witches' sabbat. Sixteenth-century engraving. Bibliothèque Nationale, Paris

quisitors brought up every angle that hinted at Joan's knowledge of sorcery and witchcraft. They tried to associate the Fairies' Tree with evil doings and pagan rites, labeling it as a meeting place for witches to hold their orgies with the Devil. They twisted Joan's innocent admission that she danced and sang there with other children at spring festivals into her joining Thursday-night witches' sabbats. She admitted that her godmother claimed to have seen a fairy at the tree but said that she herself doubted it and had never seen one. Asked if her godmother was one of the "wise women" of the village, Joan said she was a sensible, upright woman, not a witch or a sorceress.

Suddenly asked where her mandrake was, Joan replied that she had never seen one. A mandrake was a powerful narcotic herb whose root had a crude resemblance to a human being. Much superstition was attached to it—it could cure barrenness, arouse passion, and even make one rich! Joan had heard that one grew near her village, that it was dangerous and evil, and that it attracted money, but she didn't believe that. They tried to make Joan admit that her two rings—one given her by her parents, one by her brother—were sources of magic. Why else did people want to kiss her rings? Joan said she tried to prevent them but that many poor people came to her because she welcomed and helped them. Did the people believe she was sent by God? "I don't know what they believe, and I refer to their opinion; but even if they do not believe it, I am sent by God."

After this sixth session Bishop Cauchon suspended the trial for a few days in order to study the minutes and to plot future procedure. Things were not going as well as he had hoped; this sharp-witted, sharp-tongued peasant girl was proving more difficult than Cauchon had anticipated. He had not yet been able to prove her either a fraud or a heretic possessed by evil spirits. The English were growing impatient. It was decided to question Joan from now on more secretly in her own cell. Fewer inquisitors would be used, and any who had shown sympathy to Joan were ruled out. Now Joan wouldn't even have her daily short walk, which sometimes at least gave her the chance to say a prayer at the chapel door. All through the trial Joan was denied any consolation of her religion. Her only comfort was her voices, but she had little quiet time in which to hear them.

Questioning began again with only a dozen of the doctors present in her cell. From now on Joan began to weaken under the stress of the incessant hostile questioning. Physically and mentally exhausted, she began to lose some of her boldness and confidence. Her judges had already asked her time and again what sign she had given Charles to make him believe in her—everyone insisted that she had given some secret sign to the King. Her judges were going to worm it out of her somehow. Asked if there had been an angel over Charles's head when she first saw him, Joan had scornfully answered, "By St. Mary, if there was one, I did not know it, I did not see it." But her tormentors wouldn't leave this subject alone. Joan tried to resist talking about Charles at all with such words as, "You will not drag that out of me. Go and ask him." She would protect her King at all costs and never did divulge what had swayed him to accept her, nor any secret words that passed between them. They still remain a mystery.

But finally Joan was maneuvered into talking about a sign to the King. The judges' mention of an angel gave her an idea. She decided to tell a story, a sort of allegory about the

King, the crown, and an angel. Like a child making up a fairy tale, she spun an elaborate fantasy about an angel presenting the King with an indescribably beautiful crown that would last a thousand years. To one angel soon were added a host of angels who brought the crown from heaven to give to the King. She herself accompanied the angels and said to Charles, "Here is your sign, take it."

Once Joan got going she seemed to enjoy elaborating her fantasy—perhaps it was a sort of release from the grim, daily routine of her prison life and the endless questions. Though Joan got a bit mixed up between Charles's real crowning at Reims and her fantasy of the angel giving him the crown when she first met him in Chinon Castle, it was a pretty good allegory. Joan later said that she was the angel who brought the King to his crown and gave him his right to kingship. And indeed she was.

If there really was a "sign," it might simply have been Joan's promise to Charles that she would capture Orléans from the English. That she did so may have been all the proof he needed to believe in her. When Charles's churchmen in Poitiers had told Joan that they needed some sign to prove she was sent by God, she had impatiently burst out, "In the name of God, I did not come here to make signs; take me to Orléans and I will give you the signs for which I was sent." Joan's victory at Orléans could have been the sign.

Though the judges tried to paint her character as black as possible, they were unable to prove Joan immoral—her well-known virginity protected her against that accusation and they dropped the charges that her suitor had rejected her for her loose morals. But the smear remained. When they scornfully dubbed her as a lowly cowgirl, she protested that she could sew and spin as well as any woman. They were more skillful in showing her up as a heretic and not, according to them, a good orthodox Catholic. They probed her on her "sins"—dressing like a man, disobeying her parents, attempting suicide by jumping off a tower, attacking Paris on a holy feast day, and her cruelty in battle. The only instance they could dream up was her handing over the Burgundian prisoner to be tried as a criminal in the town of Lagny. Asked if she had ever seen an Englishman killed, Joan answered, "In God's name, yes. How gently you speak! Why don't they leave France and go back to their home?" This prompted a rare reaction from a visiting English lord: "Truly she is a good woman. If only she were English."

The rest of the trial centered mostly on Joan's claim that she communicated with God through her saints and on her wearing of men's clothes. These things particularly infuriated her inquisitors. They saw her spiritual independence as a threat to themselves and the Church. That she dared to bypass their judgment, saying that everything she had said or done was in God's hands, could not be tolerated. Even more maddening, Joan kept insisting she was a good Catholic, that she was devoted to the Church, and that she loved God with all her heart. The judges would have to make her understand that *they* represented the Church, that only *they* could tell if she was a good Catholic.

When they asked her if she would submit to the decision of the Church, she answered stubbornly, "I refer to God." She added that in her opinion God and the Church were one and the same. "Why," she pleaded, "do you make such difficulties?"

They tried to explain to her the rather complicated medieval

Church doctrine—the difference between the Church Militant and the Church Triumphant. The Church Militant was the Church on earth—the pope and all the clerics (themselves in fact)—and only it could judge who was acceptable as a good Catholic. Joan must submit to it or be cast out of the Church. She could not expect her soul to be saved or accepted by the Church Triumphant (which meant God and the saints in paradise) if she didn't first obey the Church Militant. Joan said she would willingly obey the Church on earth on condition she was asked nothing impossible, meaning that she would not revoke anything she had said or done by God's command and would continue to obey her voices no matter what the Church said. When asked if she was sure of salvation, she said her voices had told her she would be saved and she believed them. Asked if she believed she could not commit any sin, she said she did not know, that she relied entirely on God. The court told her that that was a weighty answer, to which Joan said, "I, too, hold it a great treasure."

Aside from the question of soul saving, the judges feared that Joan might physically escape her imprisonment through the use of sorcery and probed her on this possibility. She said that St. Catherine had told her that she would have help. She didn't know whether this meant that she would be delivered from prison or whether there might be some disturbance to help free her. She thought it would be one or the other. Joan's pathetic hope of being rescued by the townspeople did not last long.

Palm Sunday was approaching, and Joan asked to be allowed to hear mass. She was told she could only if she changed to women's clothes. She stubbornly refused, saying her male clothing did not burden her soul. Wearing men's clothes had become a symbol of Joan's independence. She not only felt them necessary for protection, but also felt they were proof of everything she had accomplished for the kingdom of France and her King, proof that she had carried out God's commands.

11

RELAPSED HERETIC

"We'll catch her yet."

On March 17 the court adjourned to draw up articles of accusation in preparation for Joan's indictment. The prosecutor, Jean d'Estivet, who was Joan's harshest judge, would read them aloud to her.

The court now convened in the room next to the great hall for a more public session with about forty of the court members, only some of whom had questioned Joan in her cell. Bishop Cauchon told Joan that their desire was not vengeance but to bring her back to the way of truth and salvation. He even offered to have one of his learned doctors advise her on how to answer questions since she was not versed in theology. Joan politely thanked him but declined his offer. "I have no intention of forsaking the counsel of God," she said. How could she count on help from these churchmen who had been tormenting her for weeks, who wouldn't believe her and often twisted her remarks? When any dared show sympathy, they were suppressed. When the English Earl of Warwick attended a session, he suspected one of the doctors was showing too much sympathy to Joan and warned the doctor that he would be thrown into the river if he tried to help that "wicked woman."

Lest there be any slipup that would prevent Joan's being condemned, the English had a written contract giving them the right to take her after the trial. Also in writing was a guarantee of pardon for all the churchmen involved in the trial should they incur any criticism. Such concern for the safety of the inquisitors suggests a certain uneasiness about the ethics of the trial.

Joan sat at a table in the center of the room to listen to the long list of her crimes, written up in seventy articles. Estivet took two days to read them. Most of them were repetitions of the earlier questions, of accusations, rumors, and tales of Joan's so-called crimes and errors of faith. Twisting many of Joan's answers, they charged her with not having been taught the true Catholic faith, but instead, "sorcery, superstitious practices, and magic arts." They accused her of keeping a mandrake in her bosom, of allowing herself to be adored, of using demons and evil spirits. Joan was allowed to reply to each accusation and in most cases flatly denied them. Often she asked the inquisitors to look at her original answers and occasionally she gave fuller ones.

Her wearing male clothes was singled out as one of her gravest sins, "abominable to God." The court's shock and horror was apparent when her male armor was described in detail. Her bearing arms in battle was "blasphemous to God," and her refusal to wear clothes suitable to her sex and womanly duties anathema to the Church. Joan angrily insisted she had never blasphemed God, and as for womanly duties, "there were enough other women to do them." And she said she would not change her clothes, even if they cut off her head.

Next came the charge that her claim to revelations was false since she gave no signs to prove them, had not sought the necessary spiritual advice of the Church, and, in fact, had kept them secret. Joan had been deceived; her voices were evil spirits, not from God. Joan defended her voices and said she would consult them as long as she lived. Asked how she summoned them, Joan said she prayed, "Most sweet God, I beg You if You love me, to reveal how I should answer these churchmen." These pleading words expressed the difficulty Joan faced throughout this trial that made so little sense to her.

The charge against Joan of putting herself above the authority of churchmen by insisting that she had direct messages from God through his saints was the most serious. The doctors contrived to link that charge with her male dress, which they decided was her way of showing defiance and refusal to submit to the Church. Finally she was charged with making no attempt to mend her ways. Joan denied that she had committed any of the crimes of which she was accused. She said she hoped she had done nothing to offend the Christian faith and she put all her trust in God.

She was taken back to her prison while the court worked out a final version of the charges, reducing the seventy to twelve. Cauchon exploded in fury when one churchman dared express some doubt as to Joan's guilt and quickly silenced him. The briefer charges, which were the basis of the final indictment, were even more damning and false than the longer articles. Without Joan ever hearing them they were sent to the University of Paris for deliberation.

Back in her cell the exhausted prisoner fell ill with vomiting and a high fever. This alarmed the English, ever fearful that

Joan might die a natural death. Warwick summoned medical doctors, who examined her and decided to bleed her. He warned them to be cautious in the bloodletting, saying, "She is sly, and might bring about her own death." D'Estivet came to see her, and Joan told him she had gotten ill from eating a carp that Cauchon had sent. D'Estivet insulted her, calling her a bawd; angry words passed between them, making Joan sicker. But Joan didn't have the good fortune to die naturally, and gradually began to recover.

In late April, when Cauchon and a few others went to see Joan, they found her still weak but by no means subdued. They had come to warn her that if she did not submit to the Church, she would be in great danger. "It seems to me," said Joan, "considering the illness I am suffering, that I am in great danger of death." And she begged to be allowed to go to confession, to take communion, and to be promised a burial in sacred ground. Cauchon said that she would first have to submit to the Church. "Whatever happens to me," said Joan, "I can do or say no other than I have already said." Warned that she would be abandoned as a heathen if she did not submit to the Church, Joan insisted she was a good Catholic and that she believed in the Church on earth, but as for her deeds and words, she repeated the same refrain: "I refer to God, who made me do everything I have done." When asked if she would submit to the Pope in Rome, Joan eagerly jumped at this opportunity. "Take me there and I will answer him." This offer to see the Pope was not sincere and was shortly withdrawn; Joan was told he was too far away, that it would be impossible. In any case it was unlikely that the Pope would have dared to oppose the University of Paris then.

Someone thought Joan was showing signs of submission and asked if he should record it. Cauchon said it was not necessary, at which Joan protested, "Ah, you write down carefully what is against me, but you do not write what is for me." Ignoring her words, the theologians still insisted that she was not submitting to the Church and that if she persisted, she would be burned at the stake as a heretic. "I will say no more," said Joan. "And if I saw the fire, I would say what I have said and nothing more."

On May 9, the usher Massieu came to conduct Joan not to the usual court assembly, but to the dungeon where she was shown instruments of torture. Cauchon and nine of the doctors, as well as the executioner, were present. They hoped that the sight of these instruments would force Joan to make a public confession of her crimes. Joan saw the terrible implements: the rack for stretching, the hooks, the pincers, and the braziers with burning coals. "Truly," she said, "if you were to tear me limb from limb and drive my soul from my body I would tell you nothing different; and if I said anything different, afterward, I would say you made me do it by force." So the doctors went into a huddle again to decide whether to apply the terrible tools or not. Some thought it the only way to break Joan's spirit; one thought it would be good for her soul. But it was finally decided not to use torture lest it blacken the prestige of this "well-run" trial. Perhaps the judges realized that torture was not likely to shake Joan's unshakeable courage.

Shortly after this, the Earl of Warwick gave an elaborate dinner party in the royal suite of the castle. Among the guests were Cauchon and Jean de Luxembourg, who had been the first to hold Joan prisoner. After wining and dining to the full, Warwick, Luxembourg, and a few other guests decided to call on Joan in her cell. Joan must have been surprised to see Jean de Luxembourg and even more surprised when he told her in a kind of sadistic joke he had come to ransom her on condition she would promise never again to bear arms against the English and Burgundians. "In God's name," said Joan, "you are making fun of me, for I know you have neither the wish nor the power." Luxembourg repeated his offer several times until Joan said, "I know well that these English will kill me, believing that after my death they will win the kingdom of France; but even if there were a hundred thousand 'goddons' they would not take the kingdom." This remark so incensed an English friend of Warwick's that he started to draw his dagger, menacing Joan. The Earl had to restrain him. Before the evening was over Warwick had words with Cauchon, telling him that the trial had lasted long enough, and that the English were growing impatient for a verdict.

After that festive evening, the trial speeded up. The University of Paris sent back its unanimous approval of the twelve articles condemning Joan. Declaring her a liar, an apostate, a heretic, the University demanded she quickly be brought to justice lest she continue to pollute and demoralize the people whom she had so long deceived.

On May 23, just a year after Joan's capture, one of the most zealous theologians read the University's verdict aloud to her. He explained that the University, the light of all knowledge, was eager for the salvation of her soul, and that it had carefully examined her words and deeds. Then he launched into his "charitable admonition," a long sermon to make her repent and return to the Catholic faith. "Joan, my dear friend," he began in honeyed words, "it is now time, at the end of your trial, to think carefully of what you have said." And he told how she had sinned by not confiding in any learned churchmen to find out the truth of her so-called revelations, which, "considering your condition and the simplicity of your knowledge, you ought to have done." And he warned her that if she did not submit to the Church, she would be punished in both body and soul. Joan remained defiant. "If I were to be condemned and saw the fire lit and the wood prepared and the executioner ready to cast me into the fire, even in the fire, I would not say anything other than what I have said. And I will maintain what I have said until death." Bishop Cauchon then declared the trial ended and said the verdict would be announced the next day. There was no doubt in his mind. Joan had proved herself a heretic. Her fate was all but sealed.

On May 24, Joan was taken outside the castle walls to a cemetery behind the Church of St. Ouen, where two wooden platforms had been set up. This first outing for Joan was not a happy one. Looking like a forlorn and disheveled child, the prisoner was led up to the smaller platform. She was thin and overwrought, worn down by months of grueling questions, and the gross treatment of her guards. With her was Massieu and a member of the University of Paris, Master Erard. On the larger platform were Bishop Cauchon and his assistants. Crowds of English had turned out to watch the dramatic scene, curious to see how Joan would react to the threat of death by burning. Excitement was already mounting at the prospect of a public execution.

Master Erard launched into his sermon on Joan's crimes, calling her an apostate, a heretic, a liar, and a witch. Directing his gaze at Joan, he told her that King Charles was a heretic too for having believed in her. Joan couldn't stand having her King insulted and she interrupted. "Speak not of my King. He is the most noble Christian of all Christians." Erard shouted to Massieu to make her be quiet. At the end of his talk he asked Joan what she had been asked a hundred times: if she would mend her evil ways and submit to the holy Church. Wearily Joan replied, as she had so many times, that she referred to God's judgment, that her words and deeds were all on His behalf, though, she added quite humbly, they were her own, not the King's nor any other's. If there were any fault in them, only she was to blame.

After exhorting her three times to repent, Erard deferred to Cauchon who began to read the sentence condemning her to death by burning. Some of the doctors were urging Joan to submit, to save her life. "Do you want to be burned alive?" they asked. Angered at the delay, an Englishman shouted, "Hurry up!" The crowd was pressing close to the platform; the noise was deafening. Erard said, "Submit now or you will end your life by fire today." Joan could see the executioner, ready with his cart. Suddenly she gave up. She would submit rather than burn. A short form of seven lines was presented to her for signing. It stated that she promised never to bear arms again, that she would cast off her male clothes, admit her sins and renounce her voices, and submit completely to Church authority. It is not known whether she understood what she was signing — she seemed to pay little attention to what she was doing. Some said she smiled, others that she laughed as she signed her name. (At some point in her short career, Joan had learned to write her name.) Her smile could have indicated hope that she would be released from her hateful English enemies.

The crowd was getting out of hand, yelling and brandishing swords, even throwing stones. In the midst of the noise and confusion, Cauchon read out the sentence: life imprisonment. Joan was "to live on the bread of sorrow and the water of affliction so that she could weep for her sins and nevermore commit them." One of the churchmen told her she had done well and had saved her soul. Joan quickly asked to be taken to a church prison, out of the hands of the English. But Bishop Cauchon coldly said, "Take her back where she came from," and once again she was led to her old cell with those same brutal English guards. All hope of better treatment was shattered.

The Earl of Warwick and the English were furious that Joan had not been condemned to death and feared their prey was escaping them. But Cauchon calmed the Earl, saying, "Don't worry. We'll catch her yet."

Back in her cell, Joan submitted to putting on women's clothes and having her head shaved in the style of a confessed penitent.

What happened in her cell in the next few days remains a mystery. Three days after her recantation, Cauchon heard a rumor that Joan had resumed wearing men's clothes, her symbol of asserting herself and defying her judges. He sent two of his assistants to confirm this, but English soldiers blocked their way and threatened to throw them in the river. There are two versions of why Joan reverted to her male dress. One was due to an act of treachery. Her guards had put her male outfit in a bag and during the night had removed her women's clothes and hidden them. When Joan woke up she asked for her clothes, and the guards threw her the bag with men's clothing. Joan protested that they knew she was forbidden to wear them, but they refused to give her anything else. So Joan lay in bed until noon when, needing to get up to use the latrine, she was forced to put on the men's clothes. The other version reported that during the night an English lord had entered her cell and tried to rape her, and that she had put on the male clothes feeling safer in them.

When Cauchon and a few of his churchmen came to see her, they found her looking miserable and outraged, her face streaked with tears. Asked why she had put on men's clothes Joan answered that she had done so of her own free will, that it was more fitting to wear men's clothes when she was surrounded by nothing but men. Another reason she gave was that the court had not kept its promise to let her hear mass or take communion while dressed as a woman. If they would allow her to go to mass, remove her chains, and put her in a church prison with women guards, she would willingly put on woman's dress. She said she would rather die than remain in chains for the rest of her life.

Then they asked her if she had heard her voices again. Joan said she had and that they had told her that she had done great wrong and damned herself by her recantation. One churchman jotted down, "Fatal answer." Joan said that she had signed the recantation purely because of her fear of the fire. She had not understood what she had signed and had never meant to deny her voices, claiming she still believed in them and that they came from God. "I told you the truth about everything as best I could," she said, and denied ever having done anything contrary to God and the Christian Church. She would rather die now than continue the agony of prison any longer.

Cauchon and his men left her, hastening off to discuss the

next step in dealing with the relapsed heretic. Cauchon met Warwick in the castle courtyard and greeted him with the words, "Be of good cheer, it is done." Then he reported to his assistants that Joan, "persuaded by the Devil," had relapsed and was wearing men's clothes again. He was ready now to carry out the law to punish the relapsed heretic.

Only three of the churchmen agreed that Joan should be sent to the stake immediately; others thought she should be given one more chance and have things better explained to her. But Cauchon and the Inquisitor, Le Maître, were the only real judges with power to sentence, and they decided that Joan would be taken to the Old Market the next morning. The stake and faggots were already in place.

At dawn of May 30, two of the doctors were sent to tell Joan of her impending death. Joan was not like herself. Weeping and in despair, she lamented, "Alas, they treat me thus cruelly . . . my body which has never been corrupted, will today be burned and turned to ashes. I would rather be beheaded seven times than burned." She remarked that had she been in a church prison this never would have happened.

Surprisingly, she was now allowed to be heard in confession and to take communion. Joan asked, "Where will I be tonight?" "Do you not have good hope in God?" asked the priest. "Yes, and with God's help I shall be in paradise," Joan responded fervently. When Cauchon later appeared in her cell, Joan confronted him. "Bishop, I die through you." He protested, explaining that she had to die because she had broken her word and returned to her evil ways.

Beyond the thick-walled castle could be heard the shouts and roars of the crowds, impatient for the show to begin. Joan, dressed in a long black shift, was led weeping from her cell and put in the executioner's cart. A pointed cap with the words "Heretic, relapsed, apostate, idolater" was placed on her shaved head. Eighty armed English soldiers accompanied the cart through the narrow cobblestone streets to the Old Market, where several platforms had been set up. On the highest one, visible to all the onlookers, was the stake surrounded by piles of wood. Visible to all too was a large sign that read, "Joan the Maid, liar, pernicious, seducer of the people, diviner, superstitious, blasphemer of God, presumptuous, misbelieving in the faith of Jesus Christ, idolater, cruel, dissolute invoker of devils, apostate, schismatic and heretic." Quite an exhaustive list of abusive insults! All the important nobles were there— the churchmen and the English lords, and as far as the eye could see crowds of people anxiously awaiting the main event. On one platform Joan faced her accusers for the last time and was subjected to one more, last sermon. Then Cauchon pronounced the final sentence. "We, by divine pity, humble bishop and brother Le Maître, deputy Inquisitor of the Faith . . . cast you forth and reject you from the communion of the Church as an infected limb, and hand you over to secular justice, praying the same to treat you with kindness and humanity in respect of your life and of your limbs."

Joan fell on her knees and began to pray, asking to be forgiven as she forgave all who had condemned her, asking too that they pray for her. Many were moved to tears, even some of the churchmen who had tormented her for so many weeks. Loiseleur, who had falsely posed as her friend, was overcome with emotion and left. Joan asked for a cross and Massieu provided a small crude one made of two sticks. She kissed it and pressed it to her breast.

Joan burned at the stake. Painting by Boutet de Monvel. Author's collection.

The English grew impatient at this emotional scene. One called out to Cauchon, "Do you mean to have us dine here?" The word was given to take her away. And without being turned over to the civil justice as she should have been, she was immediately handed over to the executioner. (The Church was allowed to condemn but not to carry out a death sentence without a civil pronouncement. This marked the final irregularity of Cauchon's trial.)

Joan was bound to the stake and the fire was lit. At her request someone brought a large crucifix from a nearby church. As the flames rose and crackled, Joan gazed at it, calling on her saints. Soon the flames enveloped her, but she could be heard calling, "Jesus, Jesus." Then silence; the freedom she had been promised had come at last.

Assured that she was dead, the executioner pushed aside the burning wood so that all could see the charred and naked body and be assured that the "witch" had not escaped. The fire was relit. Soon her ashes were gathered and thrown into the Seine River.

Even some of the English wept, and one cried out, "We are all damned; we have burned a saint."

12

AFTERWORD

"I had a daughter."

Though they burned Joan's body to ashes, they couldn't wipe out her memory. The idea that she was a witch flourished for a long time in England—even Shakespeare called her a foul "fiend," but the idea that she was a saint grew and grew among the French people. Stories flew around that Joan's heart had remained intact despite the intense fire and that, as her soul left her body, a dove flew out of the smoke!

After the trial the English dispatched letters in the name of King Henry VI to all the princes of western Christendom, stating that Joan had been put to death for the benefit of the Faith and to wipe out heresy. The University of Paris alerted the Pope and the College of Cardinals to the excellent work of Bishop Cauchon in bringing to trial and condemning to death a certain woman dressed as a man who had sinned against the orthodox faith and falsely claimed to be sent by God.

The Duke of Bedford, hoping to annul the effect of Charles's coronation, arranged to have little Henry, already King of England, crowned King of France too. But the city of Reims

A statue now rises on the spot where Joan was burned at the stake in the marketplace at Rouen. Cultural Services of the French Embassy.

refused to crown him and the English had to settle for a Paris coronation. The celebration started out with a gala procession to the cathedral of Notre Dame. As the royal cortege passed the home of the old Queen Isabella, young Henry saluted her. The doddering old queen waved back to her half-French, half-English grandson, son of her daughter and Henry V, whose marriage she and the Duke of Burgundy had arranged. She turned away in tears. One wonders what her emotions were.

The palace feast held the next day, a Sunday, was a fiasco. According to the French, the English bungled everything in what should have been an impressive ceremony. For one thing "the food was shocking." Unpardonable to the French, it had been cooked the Thursday before. And King Henry failed to bestow the expected benefits on the citizens—release of prisoners, reprieve of taxes, and gifts to the poor. The common people complained of the stinginess of the English. The whole affair was a flop; no one had a good word to say about it. No one was fooled by the coronation either. The French people knew Henry could not be a proper French King without being crowned and anointed with holy oil in the cathedral of Reims.

Then the Duke of Bedford received the worst possible setback to his schemes of English occupation. His partner, Duke Philip, noting that Charles's popularity was steadily rising, began to realize that he was French after all. In 1435, he concluded a treaty, not just a truce, with his cousin Charles, recognizing him as King of France. Charles's slow diplomacy was beginning to show results, but not without concessions. He had to give the Duke a political payback, allowing him to keep for himself many of the French lands he had captured with the aid of the English. The Duke remained as rich and powerful as ever but at least his ties with England had been severed.

Later that year the Duke of Bedford died, and soon after Paris opened its gates to Charles. The city was in shambles, suffering from the war, disrupted communications, and lack of leadership. Its neglected poor were dying off as famine stalked the city—at night wolves again swam across the Seine river to prowl the city streets in search of corpses. But now the people took new hope at the sight of a real French King who graciously pardoned them all for having supported the enemy. The fickle mob embraced the Royalists as eagerly as they had the Burgundians and the English not so long before.

Slowly but surely Charles regained power and prestige. One

evil influence on the King had been removed—his fat friend Tremoille had fallen from power. Stabbed in the stomach in an assassination attempt, Tremoille's life was saved only by his excessive flesh. He left the royal court never to return. Constable Richemont replaced him and began to step up military action against the English. Relying on the new class of rich merchants for funds, Charles built up a royal professional army with greatly improved artillery. Culverins and cannon were now effective in besieging cities. Town walls began to fall at the onslaught of French bombardments. Inspired by the memory of Joan's impetuous attacks, the French no longer waited for the English to set up barricades but took the offensive and often caught the enemy off guard or on the march. Imbued with a rising patriotic spirit, the French recaptured one by one the lands they had lost. Without Burgundy's support, the English were unable to withstand the new French vigor; enthusiasm for their "overseas" war began to wane.

Finally, in 1453, twenty-two years after Joan's death, the English were forced to leave France forever. The foreign occupation was over and, as Joan had predicted, the English went home where they belonged. Only one town, Calais, remained in English hands, another concession to Duke Philip, who wanted a base for his wool trade with England.

Shortly before this, when the town of Rouen had opened its gates to the French, the record of Joan's trial fell into Charles's hands. Almost immediately the King appointed someone to look into the proceedings, to find out on just what grounds Joan had been put to such a cruel death. With the English in retreat, Charles now felt secure enough to initiate an investigation into the trial that had condemned the Maid who had given him his crown. His councillors urged him to find a way to wipe out the "iniquitous, scandalous sentence" that cast an undesirable stigma on the King's own character. His kingship and his prestige demanded that he clear Joan in order to clear himself of any taint of heresy. Though politics and self-interest were Charles's main concern, he now showed more courage and energy than he ever had before. For he knew that any re-examination of the case would open up old animosities and might cause a clash with the Church.

Now began a long-drawn-out investigation of Joan's trial. Lasting almost seven years due to interruptions and political problems, this protracted inquiry came to be known as the Trial of Rehabilitation. First, a few of the churchmen who had participated in the first trial and were still living in Rouen were questioned. Bishop Cauchon and the prosecutor d'Estivet, Joan's implacable enemies, had died. The latter was found drowned in an open sewer, a fitting punishment, some thought, for his harsh conduct in the trial. All but one of these doctors agreed that the trial had been political, designed to prove Charles had been illegally crowned by the aid of a heretic and sorceress. Most agreed that Joan had been unfairly judged, more from fear and hate than evidence of wrongdoing. They pointed out all the irregularities of Cauchon's "beautiful trial," all the ways he and the English had attempted to intimidate any who dared disagree.

Still, Joan couldn't be cleared of her so-called crime of heresy except through the Church, which had condemned her. It was a ticklish situation for the Church to have its own members called to testify. But now that Charles was back in power, the Church needed his support. Luckily a new Pope, eager to help settle several disputes with France, agreed to look into Joan's trial. This second stage of the investigation concluded that Joan had always been a devout Catholic and that her judges had given in to English pressure to have her condemned. The trial record was shown to have been falsified in a few spots when it was translated from the daily minutes taken down in French to the Latin of the official document. Worse, the recantation Joan had signed was not the same as the one put in the official record; a longer, more incriminating one had been substituted. Though this Church inquiry found Joan innocent, no public vindication of Joan was yet made.

Not until 1455 did the final stage of the lengthy investigation take place. A more dramatic step brought Joan's own family into the limelight. Her mother, now in her eighties, appeared in Paris to petition for a rehabilitation of her daughter. With permission from the Pope, she and Joan's brothers were taken to the cathedral of Notre Dame. Joan's father had already died—it was said of a broken heart. Crowds of people were on hand and greatly moved as the old peasant woman, in tears, walked down the nave of the cathedral. Kneeling, she begged to have her daughter's honor restored and to redress the cruel injustice done to her. "I had a daughter," she said, "born in lawful marriage." She had brought Joan up in the fear of God and respect for the Church, and though her daughter had never done anything contrary to the faith, certain enemies had brought her to trial and had condemned her in a damnable and wicked way, and "put her to death most cruelly by fire."

The thoroughness of the attempt to reverse the sentence against Joan seemed never ending—inquiries were made in Domremy, in Vaucouleurs, in Orléans, every place where people had known Joan. All kinds of people, from plowman and local bell ringer to noble and priest, were interviewed. Childhood friends and relatives in Domremy testified to Joan's good character and piety. Alençon, Count Dunois the Bastard, her squire, and other fighting companions were eager to speak on Joan's behalf. Ignoring any of her failures, they emphasized only her glorious victories.

Many of her former judges who now showed up to testify were evasive and conveniently failed to remember details about the trial. But in general even they agreed that it had been unfair, based on the English terror and hatred of the girl who had changed the course of their war. Most of the judges now felt free to criticize and reveal the intimidation to which Cauchon and the English had subjected them. Of course it was easy to blame Cauchon, now that he was dead, easy to blame the English now that they had left France. Since most of the church doctors had gone along with Cauchon's verdict, they should have shared the blame. But, in a kind of cover-up, they put the blame mostly on the English and the procedure of the trial itself. Joan's mother had hoped that her daughter's judges would at least be cited for their infamous part in condemning Joan but they went scot-free.

Politics were as much a part of this trial as the first one. The judges were not completely sincere, now wanting to please their King Charles as they had formerly wanted to please the English. One exception was the University of Paris doctor Beaupère, who refused to change his former opinion and remained skeptical about Joan's revelations. He thought they were "more from human intention than supernatural," and that "she was very subtle, with a woman's subtlety." Beaupère was one of the many medieval churchmen who thought women were the source of all evil.

Whatever the politics, the results of this Rehabilitation Trial were clear. In 1456, the trial condemning Joan was pronounced null and void because of fraud and errors. Joan was cleared of heresy. Charles could rest assured that he had no taint of guilt by association with a heretic. The verdict of this retrial was read aloud to crowds of people in the Old Market of Rouen, at the very spot where Joan had been burned. One copy of the original trial record was publicly and dramatically torn up.

But no mention was made of that difficult problem—Joan's claim to visions—nor of her achievements. The Church still reserved the right to examine visionaries and to pronounce whether they were true or false. It is unlikely that Joan would have accepted anyone's judgment on her voices except her own. She was so convinced of their reality that they became the very meaning of her life. Joan had clashed more with Church authorities than with the Church itself. She wholeheartedly believed in the Church but in her own way. She did not agree when the men who judged her said that only *they* could decide the truth. She had her own inner truth. Her religion, uncluttered by the rigid rules and scholastic jargon of her judges, was simple and direct. And many of the doctors must have inwardly realized that she was a true believer in the faith. Her deep sincerity was obvious.

With her name cleared and her sentence revoked, the cult of Joan as heroine and saint grew and grew among the people. She became a folk heroine who had saved the kingdom of France. But almost five hundred years went by before the Church and state recognized her as a saint. In 1920 she was canonized, for her virtuous life and her faith in God. There was no mention of her heroism, her visions, or her courage.

Joan was spared knowing the strange fate of her beloved saints Margaret and Catherine, who have been removed from the Church calendar because of doubts that they ever existed! But even such a disillusionment would not have destroyed her faith in her revelations and her mission.

The French writer and statesman André Malraux has best expressed how the people who never ceased to love and admire her, felt. *"O, Jeanne, sans sépulchre et sans portrait, toi qui savais que le tombeau des héros est le cœur des vivants,"* which can be freely translated as "Oh, Joan, without any grave or portrait to remember you by, you who knew that the true monument for heroes is in the hearts of the living."

AUTHOR'S NOTE

Though we don't know what she looked like, we know more about Joan's character than about any other woman who lived before the modern age. And what we know comes largely from her own words in the trial that condemned her and from the people who knew and testified about her in the retrial that cleared her. The men who condemned Joan never would have dreamed how valuable her Trial Record would be to posterity. Translated into modern French at the end of the last century, it became available to the world and brought Joan to life through her own words, revealing her extraordinary courage, her intelligence and sincerity. The Trial was her greatest challenge and showed her in a new kind of glory.

Joan has inspired more books than any other woman in history. Her fame is worldwide. Yet despite her fame and the enormous fund of information about her, Joan remains an enigma with many questions about her still unanswered. This is part of the fascination of writing about her — trying to break through the layers of myths and legends in order to find the real Joan.

My attempt to find Joan is best expressed in her own words toward the end of her trial: "I have tried to tell the truth in everything as best I could." But I make no claims to final answers.

Joan has also inspired many different interpretations. One writer thought Joan actually belonged to a witch cult, that her male clothing was a sign of her membership. Others have thought she was psychotic and subject to hallucinations. One saw her as an innocent tool of conspirators. A few have made fun of her but even so could not fail to admire her heroism. Many have thought she must have been of royal blood to have answered her trial judges so intelligently. Some have even insisted she was an illegitimate half sister to Charles! A few, like the dramatist George Bernard Shaw, have thought Joan an early Protestant. But Joan was neither a reformer nor against the Catholic faith, in which she deeply believed and whose rituals she carefully observed. Most writers have accepted Joan as the peasant girl who became the savior of France, the heroine who inspired new patriotic spirit among the French people to save their kingdom and their King from outside invasion. In World War I, a popular song, "Joan of Arc, They Are Calling You," was widely sung by French and American troops seeking her inspiration to lead them to victory. She is and deserves to be France's most popular heroine and saint.

In the five hundred years since her death, Joan has been used as a symbol for many different causes. Her image has changed with changing times. In a way she has been reinvented by each new generation to suit new attitudes and new ideals. She has been called on by such extreme opposites as communism and monarchism, each claiming her as their champion. She has come to mean all things to all people.

Extolled in poetry, music, opera, drama, dance, and art, the name of Joan of Arc is known to every schoolchild. Yet the myths and legends told of her in children's books have often frozen her into a mold, a sort of plastic saint in shining armor on a white war-horse, or an innocent little girl tending sheep in an idyllic meadow, a fairy-tale character without flesh and blood.

With the abundance of information about Joan, each biographer has to decide how to interpret her character and her amazing life, which does indeed read like a fairy tale with a sad ending. Joan's life was so brief—her public career lasted only a little over a year—that it might seem an easy task. But in fact, the more you study her, the more you run into questions.

For some, the most difficult problem to explain is her "voices" —even though they were no problem for her contemporaries, who worried only where they came from, God or the Devil. One can't begin to understand Joan without understanding the credulous age in which she lived.

In the fifteenth century the supernatural was close to people. In that prescientific era men and women turned to the supernatural for help and for explanations of natural disasters and the ills of society. Today we rely more on science to explain much that was inexplicable to medieval people.

I think of Joan as a very pious girl, dedicated to the Catholic folk religion of her countryside. Even if the folk religion differed from that of the established Church, incorporating as it did old Celtic beliefs and customs, it was not any less religious or less spiritual. After all, many people find God in nature. I believe that Joan was so sure she was in touch with the supernatural, that it directed her whole life. Much as a little child believes in Santa Claus, Joan sincerely believed in the reality of the saints whose statues she could see and before which she could pray. I do not doubt her sincerity in believing that her saints brought her messages from God, convincing her that He had chosen her for a great mission.

Joan had her first vision when she was thirteen, an age when girls often have dreams of missionary zeal, of doing something heroic for some good cause. I think that Joan, surrounded by the horrors of war and instilled with a passionate loyalty to the French monarchy, had a burning desire to do something to alleviate the misery of her country. Her longing became an obsession, which led to visions. And her visions gave her the courage to carry out her mission. When she was asked how she knew it was St. Michael who spoke to her, her answer, "I had the will to believe it," is, I think, a clue to her career. Her desire and her will to believe gave her the courage to try what seemed impossible, especially for a peasant girl of no standing and of no education—a seemingly ordinary child in her own village. That she could persuade the discouraged French royal court and the apathetic Charles to trust her, and that she succeeded in fulfilling most of her mission, is what seems miraculous to me. I think that some of the miracles ascribed to her, like the one that credits her with bringing a baby back to life, were probably the creations of her followers, who believed that everything she did was a miracle. Other miracles attributed to her, like recognizing Charles and changing the wind and current of the Loire River, can be explained in a nonsupernatural way. Joan herself is not so easy to explain. She is more of a miracle than the many miracles attributed to her.

Yet I find her a very *human* human being, a unique combination of a practical, earthy peasant girl and a pious, inspired heroine.

She was not the gentle, saintly type of mystic who sought to reform the morals of society, to save men's souls from sin. Joan's goal was heroic, to save her country and her King by fighting with courage and spirit.

Only in one way did Joan resemble other female mystics— she had visions. Even though her visions were of a military sort, they were just as real to her as visions were to other more ecstatic female mystics. The only way a female with strong convictions on public events could be heard, in that male-oriented society, was to claim some visionary experience or prophetic power. Only then would she be listened to. I doubt that Joan was conscious of this but, nonetheless, I think her revelations gave her the chance to be believed. Stating that she had come at God's command to rescue France gave her recognition, made her the leader for whom all loyal French were waiting. Her virginity, so prized in those days, not only gave her prestige, but also helped her in a practical way. Had she been married or pregnant or a mother, she never would have been allowed to go to war.

Joan often had to struggle against her own very human reactions in order to stick to her God-sent mission. With the people's adulation, it was hard not to let power go to her head, as she once admitted. She had a weakness for finery and was proud of her gorgeous armor, which was quite natural if more worldly than expected of a God-inspired girl. After the coronation, she was perhaps too sure of herself and took matters into her own hands. Such arrogance lost her the support of the Archbishop of Reims, and Charles seemed to lose faith in her too. She suffered a terrible letdown after the coronation and reacted in a reckless, if human, way, sometimes losing her temper and her patience, attacking Paris without full royal backing. After being captured and held prisoner, she once gave way to despair, even disobeyed her voices by jumping off the tower of Beaurevoir Castle. And just before her final punishment, she admitted her very real physical fear of death by burning. She did not seek a martyr's death, but nonetheless she suffered one.

The fact that Joan had to struggle to overcome some human weaknesses makes her, for me, all the greater as a human being, and makes her achievements all the more remarkable. I agree with the writer who said, "She is entirely human—and never was humanity greater."

BIBLIOGRAPHY

❧

Biographies and Studies of Joan of Arc

Barstow, Anne L. *Joan of Arc: Heretic, Mystic, and Shaman.* Lewiston, ME: E. Mellen Press, 1986.

A feminist and religious point of view. New, interesting interpretation.

Gies, Francis. *Joan of Arc: The Legend and the Reality.* New York: Harper & Row, Publishers, 1981.

A good, straightforward, accurate account.

Lang, Andrew. *The Maid of France: Being the story of the life and death of Jeanne d'Arc.* London: Longmans, Green, 1922.

Very sentimental.

Lucie-Smith, Edward A. *Joan of Arc.* New York: W. W. Norton & Company, Inc., 1976.

Psychological approach.

Marot, Pierre. *Joan the Good Lorrainer at Domrémy.* French ed.: Paris: Éditions Alpina, 1951.

Good on Joan's childhood background.

Pernoud, Régine. *Joan of Arc: By Herself and Her Witnesses.* Translated into English by E. Hymans. New York: Stein & Day, Publishers, 1966.

Written by a leading French historian.

———. *The Retrial of Joan of Arc.* Translated by J. M. Cohen. New York: Harcourt Brace, 1955.

One of the few books on the rehabilitation trial.

Sackville-West, Vita. *Saint Joan of Arc*. Garden City, NY: Doubleday, Doran & Company, Inc., 1936.

> Wonderful, if dated, evocation of Joan's character.

Shaw, George Bernard. *Saint Joan*. Baltimore: Penguin Books, Inc., 1924.

> The greatest drama about Joan.

Warner, Marina. *Joan of Arc: The Image of Female Heroism*. New York: Alfred A. Knopf, Inc., 1981.

> A study of the different interpretations and the changing image of Joan for the last five hundred years.

Williams, Jay. *Joan of Arc*. New York: American Heritage Publishing Company, Inc., 1963.

> Especially for young people, loaded with illustrations, well written.

Books in English on the Trial of Joan of Arc

Barrett, W. P. *The Trial of Jeanne d'Arc*. Translated into English from original Latin and French documents. New York: Gotham House, 1932.

Scott, W. S. *The Trial of Joan of Arc*. London: Folio Society, 1956.

> English translation of original French minutes of the trial.

Trask, Willard. *Joan of Arc: Self-Portrait*. New York: Stackpole Sons, 1936.

> Joan's own words from her trial records without the judges' questions and without any interpretation.

Background Material—History and Culture of the Fifteenth Century

Huizinga, J. *The Waning of the Middle Ages: A Study of the Forms of Life, Thought and Art in France and the Netherlands in the Dawn of the Renaissance*. Garden City, NY: Anchor Books, 1954.

———. *Men and Ideas*. Pp. 207–239. New York: Meridian Book Inc., 1959.

> Essay on Joan of Arc and criticism of G. B. Shaw's interpretation of Joan and her trial. Huizinga is justly famous for his ability to convey the feeling and texture of the fifteenth century.

Lightbody, C. W. *The Judgments of Joan: A Study in Cultural History*. Cambridge, MA: Harvard University Press, 1961.

> Explains the society in which Joan lived.

Oman, C. W. C. *The Art of War in the Middle Ages*. Ithaca, NY: Cornell University Press, 1953.

Short, clear, with details of important battles.

Seward, Desmond. *The Hundred Years War: The English in France, 1337–1453.* New York: Atheneum Publishers, 1978.

Lively, clear account of the war.

Wadier, Roger. *Conteurs du Pays de Jeanne d'Arc.* Vicherey: R. Wodier, 1985.

Written in French. An interesting folklore of Joan's countryside — beliefs, customs, songs, etc.

INDEX

❧

Italic type indicates illustrations

Index

Index

English longbows, 75, 76
Epidemics, 10
Erard, Master, 141–42
Escape attempts, 106, 122
Escorts of Joan, 36–37, 38–39
   advance on Orléans, 49–51
Estivet, Jean d', 115, 135, 136, 138,
   death of, 153
Examination of Joan, 44–46
Exorcism of Joan, 36

Fairies, belief in, 23
Fairies' Tree, *22*, 22–23
   trial questioning, 129
Faith, trial questions, 121
Falstaff (Shakespeare character), 77
Family of Joan, 17–18, 27–28, 154
   at coronation, 83
Famine, 10
Farm life, 21
Fashions, fifteenth-century, 46–48, *47*
Fastolf, Sir John, 61, 73, 74–75
   battle of Patay, 76–77
Father of Joan, 17–18, 27–28, 154
Female visionaries, 163
Fertility rites, 23
Fierbois, St. Catherine's Chapel, 39–40,
   48–49
Fifteenth-century France, 3–13, 161
Flavy, Guillaume de, 101–3
Folk religion, 19–20, 22–23, 114, 161–62
Fortified gateway, Vaucouleurs, *32*
Fountain, Sacred, 22
France, fifteenth-century, 3–13, 161
French army, military tactics, 75–76
French national emblem, 7
French people, and Treaty of Troyes, 7

Garden of the Fairies, 19
Gilles de Rais, 50
God, communication with, trial
   questions, 132
Godfather of Joan, 82

Godmother of Joan, 22
Grand Inquisitor, 114–15
Great Schism, 9–10

Harassment of Joan, in prison, 117, 122
Hats, fifteenth-century, 46–48, *47*
Healing arts, 23
   Joan and, 35
Heart of Joan, 149
Hell, artistic portrayals, 12
Helmeted head, *73*
Henry V, King of England, 6–7
   death of, 12
Henry VI, King of England, 12, 113
   French coronation, 149–51
Herbs, healing, 23
Heresy, 10, 111
   fears of, 109–10
   trial for, 114, 116–18
Heretic, 119, 130, 140
Holy day attack on Paris, 94
Home of Joan, 15–17, *16*
Horses given to Joan, 34, 35, 36, 44
Hundred Years' War, 6

Illness of Joan, in prison, 137–38
Imprisonment of Joan, 104–11
   by English, 113
   See also Trial of Joan
Independence, spiritual, 132
Infant, revival of, 100
Inquisition, 114–15, 117–18
Insanity of Charles VI, 3–4
Interior of peasant house, *17*
Interpretations of Joan, 160–61
Irregularities of Joan's trial, 113–14, 148
Isabella, Queen of France, 4, 6, 12, 30,
   81, 150
   Treaty of Troyes, 7

Jacques d'Arc (father of Joan), 17–18,
   154
   dream about Joan, 27–28
Jargeau (town), 71–73

Index

ABOUT THE AUTHOR

POLLY SCHOYER BROOKS is the author of the widely praised *Queen Eleanor*, as well as a series of history books for teenagers written with her co-author, Nancy Zinsser Walworth. A long-time interest in education, dating back to her student days at Radcliffe, has led her to teach at the Dalton Schools and to help develop curricula for the New Canaan, Connecticut, school system. Mrs. Brooks lives in New Canaan and keeps in touch with her four grown children and nine grandchildren.